The Human Idea

Earth's Newest Ecosystem

The Human Idea
©2024 Anne Riley

All rights reserved. No part of this publication may be reproduced, distributed, or transmitted in any form or by any means, including photocopying, recording, or other electronic or mechanical methods, without the prior written permission of the publisher, except in the case of brief quotations embodied in critical reviews and certain other noncommercial uses permitted by copyright law. For permission requests, write to the publisher, addressed "Attention: Permissions Coordinator:" at the address below:

Anne Riley
Montgomery, IL
Thehumanideasphere@gmail.com

Ordering Information:
Special discounts are available on quantity purchases by corporations, associations, educational institutions, and others. For details, contact A.L. Willingham above.

Printed in the United States of America

First Edition

Softcover ISBN 978-1-66641-062-4
Ebook   ISBN 978-1-66641-063-1

LCCN: 2024945113

Publisher
Winsome Entertainment Group LLC
Murray. UT

To Tim
I love to laugh with you

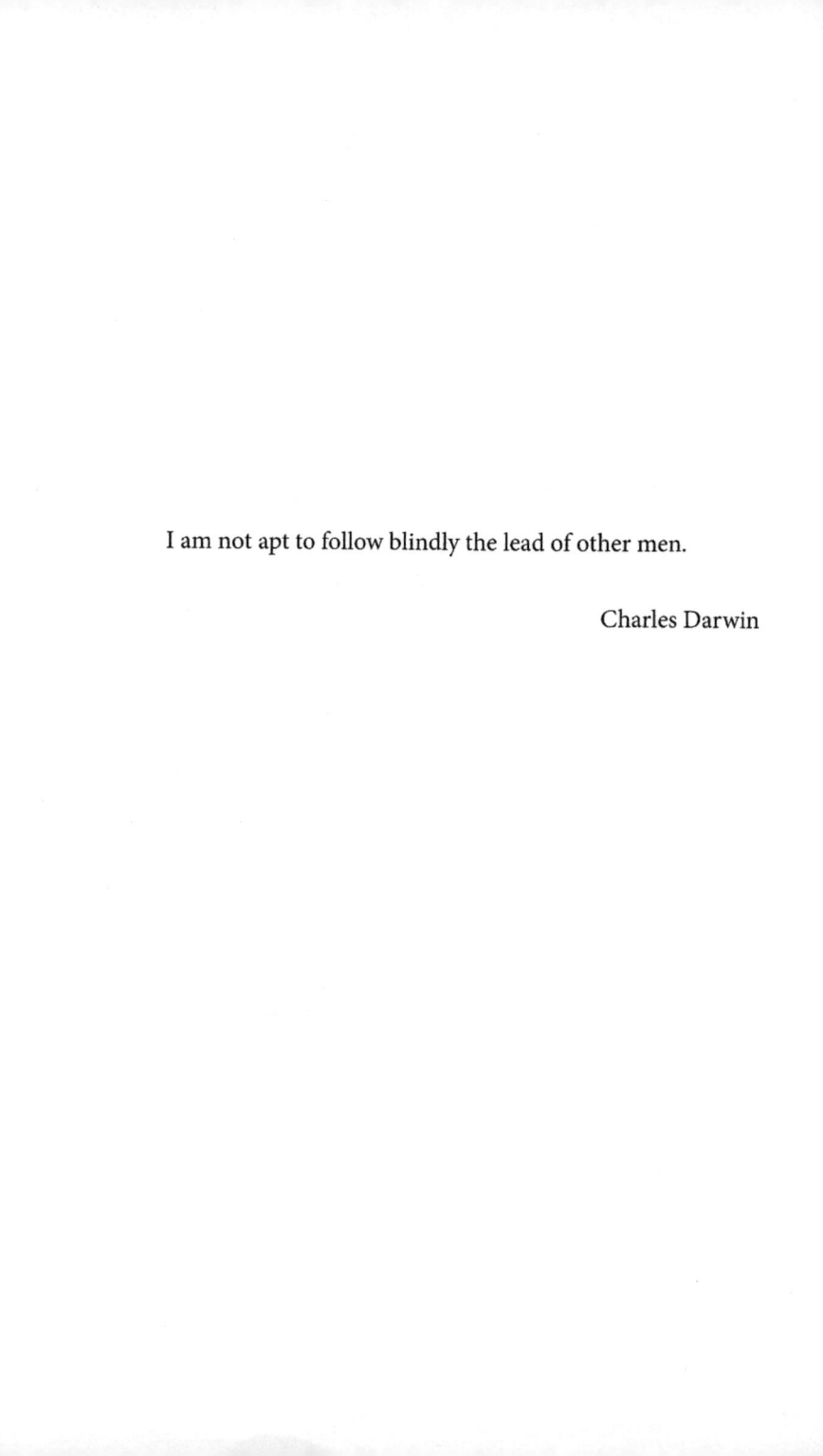

I am not apt to follow blindly the lead of other men.

Charles Darwin

Table of Contents

Author's Note 1

Introduction 3

PART 1 ECOSYSTEM 0 Energy and Matter

Note: this is NOT an ecosystem 13

1. Energy 15

2. Environment 26

3. Life 32

PART 2 ECOSYSTEM 1 DNA and the Cell 39

4. The Characteristics of Life 41

5. Competition 58

6. Collaboration 65

7. Coordination 75

8. Information 87

9. The World Before Humans 97

PART 3 ECOSYSTEM 2 The Ideasphere 101

10. Humans 103

11. Human Information 112

12. Human Information Processing 121

13. Characteristics of Human Life 127

14. Human Competition	142
15. The Effects of Human Competition	152
16. Human Collaboration	166
17. Human Coordination	179
18. The Nature of Human Coordination	191
19. The Idealsphere	201
20. Solutions	208
21. Next . . .	244
Appendix 1: A Few More Details About RNA And DNA	248
Appendix 2: The Ideasphere: A Practical Application: Social Media	253
Sources	264
Afterword	305
Acknowledgments	308
About the Author	310

Author's Note

In this book, I describe a new way to look at humanity. The facts are not new, but the synthesis of the facts is new. Out of the vast number of facts that scientists have, over thousands of years, determined are true, I use only a small subset to make my case. I do not pretend, and do not want you to think that I am disregarding the rest. It is just that when dealing with a subject at the 30,000-foot level, the minute details can cloud the main points I want to convey. For example, I might say that an elephant is gray. That is only one aspect of an elephant. It has giant ears and ivory tusks and a trunk and many other qualities. But I am going to stick to the main, and true, point that the elephant is gray in order to make my argument about how the elephant fits into the natural world. There are many aspects of the universe, the earth, life and humans I will leave out. This is intentional so that I can magnify the points about the universe, the earth, life and humans I do want you to understand.

This universe is not black and white. For every fact I discuss, there are exceptions. Yes, DNA is the source of almost all life, but there are a few RNA organisms out there too. At times, I will emphasize a particular point, but please remember, nature runs on a continuum and there are many versions of things. For instance, I make a point that non-humans follow the directions as specified in their DNA and cannot choose. There are gradations of this aspect in life forms. Humans are ultra choosers. No other species can choose even remotely like humans can. So, please understand that when I make these statements I am comparing a natural quality to a human quality on a relative basis.

Now, you are free to read, and I hope, enjoy.

Introduction

Why are we here on Earth?

Humans have been asking this question for thousands of years. We are still asking it today. The answer is important, of course. But in seeking the answer, we often miss the most essential aspect of the question: How are we humans able to ask this question? No other creature that we know of on this planet even cares about this question or the answer. They are here. They exist. They live each moment until they die.

So, let me ask another question: Why do humans ask why they exist?

We haven't had much success in answering the first question, so do we have any hope of answering the second? Are we destined to live with unanswered questions forever?

I contend that these questions can indeed be answered. We've just been looking for the explanations in the wrong place. To find the answer to any question, we must always start at a foundation where truth actually exists and proceed from there.

From the beginning, people have aspired to answer these questions from the human perspective. But from the human perspective alone, it's impossible to discern a satisfactory answer. Our efforts have spawned multiple religions and philosophies, and we still have no definitive answer. So, we must go deeper. We must examine life before humans existed.

Let us think of all living beings as a single group—the life group. If we adjust our perspective to view the world from this angle, we can see that life forms have lived on this planet in an unbroken chain for about 3.8 billion years. Over time, they underwent systemic and structural changes. They survived meteor strikes, volcanic explosions, and drastic weather changes. Even though many members of the life group died along the way, some always survived to keep the chain of existence unbroken.

So, why does life exist? What has enabled life to survive for so long? We humans tend to focus on separate species: How many legs do they have? How do they live? What do they eat? How do they die? Next. But when we ask these discrete questions about specific life forms, we miss the broader picture. How did life start? Why has life itself never gone extinct? Life is resilient. Life is tough. Life keeps going. Why? I contend that the answers to these questions are the key to understanding how humans can survive and thrive.

Scientists have amassed an enormous amount of knowledge about how this world operates. Astronomers have unlocked the secrets of the Big Bang and have mapped innumerable galaxies spread across the universe. Physicists have discovered the inner workings of atoms and how energy moves as gravity and electromagnetism and nuclear forces. Biologists have unlocked the secrets of the human cell and have ascertained the workings of DNA, which is present in all life forms. Chemists and geologists and paleontologists and meteorologists and . . . I could go on. The point is, people have studied all aspects of this world we live in, and they have discovered a lot, and I mean *a lot*, about how it all works. Have they learned everything there is to know? Of course not. But have they deciphered enough for us to be able to make sense of the whole picture? Do we know enough to piece together the story of life and humans in a comprehensible way? Can we draw a throughline from the Big Bang to humans that serves as a guide to how we can survive?

I say the answer to these questions is a resounding yes.

Abraham Lincoln once said, "Be sure you put your feet in the right place, then stand firm." That is how we must start if we truly want to understand humans. We must root ourselves firmly in fact. And where are the facts? They are present in all the findings our scientists have made about the natural world, which have been repeatedly validated over time. This is where we must start—with the basic truths we know about life.

Anchoring ourselves in the facts and truth of the natural world is essential, because when we begin to discuss humans, the first thing we find is that humans are super strange. They come from a long lineage of life, but they act very differently than all other life forms. Humans' unusual abilities have radically changed life as it had existed for 3.8 billion years. Yet nothing ever derives from nothing. Humans may have changed the game, but they didn't invent it. They have inherited every aspect of their lives from their nonhuman ancestors. They need resources to survive. They use the same survival tools. They die like every other being does. Humans may be odd, but they are not original. Once we understand how nonhumans have successfully survived for billions of years, we can examine how humans differ from their ancestors. Once we know how humans differ, we can understand how humans diverged from the successful behavior of their ancestors and determine how to correct our course.

Why is this important? Well, humans have been wildly successful in their survival efforts so far. Humans have produced billions of offspring. They have manipulated the earth's natural resources in amazingly inventive ways. They have learned to process and spread information at blinding speed. They've developed complicated human systems: political, economic, cultural, business, and religious, to name a few.

Now, things are changing. We are coming to a turning point. Millions of humans are starving on any given day. The environment is responding to human activity with erratic natural events, such as increased global temperatures, wildfires, and floods. Information is being spread without regard to its veracity. Massive wealth inequality is having a dramatic effect on the well-being of most humans living on Earth.

I contend that we humans never applied the successful survival strategies of our ancestors. How could we? We never knew the strategies. The facts that scientists have uncovered have become known only recently. We didn't know anything about any survival strategies when we arrived on this earth as Homo sapiens around 200,000 or so years ago. We just found ourselves on this earth with different capabilities, and we did what all other animals did: we lived. But because we have different abilities, we lived differently and immediately began to manipulate this world in some very unusual ways.

It is in this "living differently" that humanity has proven to be a double-edged sword. What makes humans different from all creatures that existed before? What makes us ask, "Why?" Why do we exist? Why do we ask why we exist?

Because we can think. We can create ideas.

It is the human idea that is the source of the profound difference between humans and every other life form that exists on earth. Our ability to conjure up an idea and put it into action is unique to humans and has changed the course of natural history. So, if we want to understand humans, we must start with the human idea.

Is it possible to know the nature of humans without the benefit of religion or philosophy? Well, nature has existed a long time without the need for either of these human constructs. I believe that at its core, nature is deceptively simple. All life forms use the same basic rules to survive. But because the life forms that use these simple rules keep getting more and more complex as time goes on, it gets more difficult to sort out the unadulterated truths from all the weird, complicated, and unusual ways those simple truths are displayed.

This book pulls together the pertinent facts that our scientists have discovered about nonhuman survival. It then extrapolates those facts to humans and discusses how we use the tools we were born with in a very different way because of our ability to create ideas. Lastly, the book describes how humans can put this knowledge into practice to build a better world.

To make a comprehensive case, to really understand humans and their ideas, we must first rearrange the facts that our scientists have given us so that we can see the patterns of life. Instead of viewing Earth's ecosystem as a vast web of interconnected species, which it is, let us adjust our perspective. Let us look at the ecosystem as a set of concentric circles. At the very core of our circle is DNA, the information that makes life possible on Earth. A genome is collection of DNA molecules that defines the instructions a particular life form uses to survive. Every plant and animal on Earth, including humans, has a unique genome. The cell contains the genome along with a myriad of parts that enable the cell to live, that is, to function as a life form. Cells are the basic unit of life on Earth. All living is done by cells. Over time, cells have evolved to join together to form tissues and organs. These tissues and organs have developed to make complex bodies like bees and tigers and humans. When we look at the ecosystem this way, we can begin to see life's story; we can see how life formed and evolved over time with each level of complexity building from the level below. We can also begin to parse out the clues that enabled living beings to survive even as their structures changed over time. This is what the ecosystem looks like when viewed as a set of concentric yet related units:

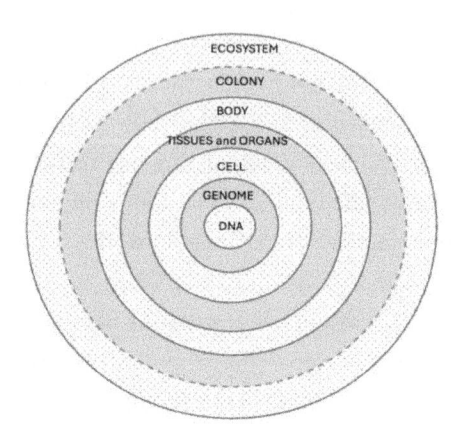

When humans emerged with their ideas, they created a brand-new ecosystem. I call it the ideasphere. Unsurprisingly, it looks very similar to the natural ecosystem from which it emerged, but at its core is the human idea, the information that makes human life unique.

Unlike DNA, ideas are not physical. They do not have any real meaning until they can be converted into a physical representation. For instance, I can think about human ideas, but until I actually convert my ideas into a form that physically exists and can be shared with others, it doesn't actually exist in any useful way. I can write a book, or make a documentary, or create an audiobook, any physical form will do. Other life forms can't do this to the extent humans can. Bees can build hives, and birds can build nests, but these actions are the result of long inherited instructions that have promoted survival rather than the result of creative thought.

The ideasphere is a parallel construction to the ecosystem. Like a genome, the mind is a collection of ideas that define the actions a particular human uses to survive. A human contains the genome along with a myriad of parts that enable a person to put those ideas into physical form. Humans are the basic unit of life in the ideasphere. All living is done by humans. Over time, humans have evolved to join together to implement different ideas. We call these groups institutions. Unlike organs in the ecosystem, institutions do not make up a society. It is people, and people alone, that form a society. Some societies have joined together as formal multinational groups. The European Union is a prime example. Above that level is a world society. Humans do not currently operate in a single world society, although it is possible for us to do so. A "world society" of animals is not possible because animals have only very limited ways to communicate with each other. But because humans have been able to use their ideas to develop means of communication, it is definitely within the capability of people to develop a world society. This is what the ecosystem looks like when viewed as a set of concentric yet related units.

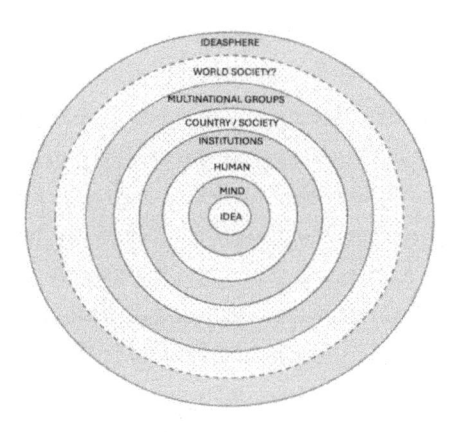

```
IDEASPHERE
  WORLD SOCIETY?
    MULTINATIONAL GROUPS
      COUNTRY / SOCIETY
        INSTITUTIONS
          HUMAN
            MIND
              IDEA
```

When we look at the human ecosystem this way, we can begin to see where and how humans have diverged from their predecessors. We can see how humans used ideas to develop more complex ways to interact with each level building from the level below. We can start to see how humans use the very same tools all life forms use to survive. We can also get a glimmer of how humans used these survival tools differently than their predecessors.

The human idea gives people choice about how to apply life's rules. Animals have no such luxury. They can only apply the rules that they have inherited from billions of years of evolution, and which have long proved to ensure survival. Our human bodies know these rules and apply them so our bodies can live. But it is ironic that our human minds do not know these rules. We are born with no ideas. How we can apply rules we do not know? And so, we have fumbled along in our newly formed ecosystem without a clue as to how to proceed.

Our human record on successful survival is mixed. We have implemented wonderful and amazing and awe-inspiring ideas throughout our history. We have also implemented deadly, cruel and destructive ideas throughout our history. And now, we are at the cusp of an existential threat to our actual physical existence in the form of human induced climate change.

I end the book by connecting the way individual life forms ensure their survival to how humans can enhance their chance of survival. Cells have developed very specific structures and perform very specific actions to make sure they survive. Humans can learn by understanding these structures and actions and applying them to human life. The translation, however, is not direct. It cannot possibly be. Human ideas work too differently. We must convert the natural world's "automatic" successful survival strategies, so they are compatible to humans and their ideas. I call this version of the human ecosystem, the "idealsphere." I probably don't need to tell you this, but we need some serious and fundamental changes if we hope to be as successful as our predecessors, that is, if we hope to create an "idealsphere."

So, let's begin. To understand humans, we need to start at the beginning. The very beginning. As we proceed, keep in mind our concentric circles. The universe has its concentric circles, too, though we don't know the details as well as we know those of life on Earth. But the patterns are the same at every level. Ready?

PART 1

ECOSYSTEM 0

The Universe: Energy and Matter

Note: This is a system but NOT an ecosystem

Chapter 1
Energy

In the beginning there was . . . energy. In the end there will be . . . energy. And all the time in between, including the moment we are living right now, is filled with . . . energy. We are all just different forms of energy.

The U.S Energy Information Administration describes energy as "the ability to do work." Let's rearrange that idea just a bit. Let's define energy as the capacity to move. To do work, something must move, so we can think of energy as movement. Energy moves. In the beginning, at the time of the Big Bang, energy exploded outward with great velocity. In less than a second, some of the energy was converted into forces—what we call gravity and electromagnetism. The early universe was extremely hot, and these energy particles moved fast, but they lost their initial velocity relatively quickly. As they moved away from each other, they slowed down, and the universe began to cool. When the energy particles slowed down, collisions became possible, which further disrupted the outward trajectory of the particles. Think of a man driving 30 mph on the expressway. He's moseying along, minding his own business, looking at the road signs in the hope of finding a rest area, when—wham!—a speeding vehicle smashes into the rear of his car. Now, if the speeding car is going fast enough, say 180 mph, it may just bounce off the slower car and continue on its way. But if the speeding car is going a bit slower, the cars may not be able to come apart. In that case, they proceed down the highway as a crunched-together unit until they slow to a stop. And depending on the conditions at the time, many other things could happen. They could veer off the highway. One vehicle could get smashed while the other could be relatively unscathed. One driver could shimmy out the window and flee the scene. Another vehicle could come along and smash into the mess, making it an even bigger mess. The variations are endless.

This is how the particles in the early universe worked, except the "cars" were teeny energy particles and moved much, much faster. Each time collisions occurred, the particles would either bounce off each other, join together, or do one of countless other possible actions in between.

At first, the outcomes of the collisions were pretty simple. With so much heat and speed, the energy particles mainly bounced off each other. But as the universe cooled, all kinds of "in-between" particles began to form. Scientists identify these as subatomic particles—little pieces of energy that flew around and eventually collided together. One of the results of these collisions was matter.

Matter is a particularly interesting form of energy. Some physicists devote all their research time to blowing up atoms, the tiniest stable matter units, so they can peek inside and see what they're made of. We can draw some basic conclusions from their work, even as they continue to broaden their knowledge every day. Matter is not just another form of energy; it is a really stable form of energy. The atom's nucleus is composed of high-speed force particles and slower subatomic matter particles all mixed together and held in place by extremely strong forces. Scientists call them the "strong nuclear force and the weak nuclear force." The nucleus is held together so tightly that it takes a massive amount of energy to rip it apart. As the universe cooled and energy particles flew farther apart, these matter particles found themselves stuck together in areas where there was insufficient energy to tear them apart. It took 380,000 years for the universe to cool enough to produce hydrogen—the very first atom and the basis of all visible matter in the universe. Hydrogen is an atom with one proton and one neutron in its nucleus. An electron rotates around the nucleus held in place by the electromagnetic force.

Matter holds a lot of energy. Using Einstein's equation, $E = mc^2$, which identifies the relationship between mass and energy, we can calculate that a pound of matter contains roughly four quintillion calories ($4 * 10^{18}$). Believe me, that's a lot.

Matter may be stable, but it is still a form of energy. And what does energy do? It moves. Hydrogen atoms floated around the universe and attracted each other via the force of gravity trapped within their nuclei. When hydrogen atoms drew very close together, a fight ensued. On one side, the gravity drew the atoms toward each other. On the other, the nuclear forces inside the atom resisted gravity's pressure. A standoff occurred. If enough hydrogen atoms joined the party, there came a point where the nuclear forces could no longer hold, and gravity would win. When that happened, the hydrogen atoms would rapidly collapse. The force of the collapse would be so great that the electrons would be torn off the atom and fly outward, emitting light as they flew. The nuclei of the hydrogen atoms would then be squeezed together, where they regrouped as helium atoms with two protons and two neutrons with even stronger nuclear forces now holding them together. That would reset the balance point. Gravity would now have to exert much more force to break apart this new matter configuration.

What I have just described is a star. Stars are made of hydrogen that is collapsing due to the gravitational pressure on their atoms. Scientists call the process where hydrogen atoms join together to make helium "fusion." This is how some heavier elements were formed too. When some gigantic stars run out of fuel altogether, they explode under gravitational pressure and create a supernova. Supernovas are responsible for producing all the elements heavier than iron. You might be interested to know that all elements larger than helium make up only 2% of all visible matter in the universe. Today, 13.8 billion years after the Big Bang, hydrogen still makes up 92% of all visible matter in the universe; helium adds 6%.

We see this concentric pattern repeatedly in the universe. Energy in the form of tiny force particles collide to make subatomic matter particles. These new particles then combine to make energy units we call atoms. As time goes on, the atoms coalesce to become larger elements. In this book, we are primarily concerned about energy in the form of matter, but remember, it's all energy. We are all, when it comes right down to it, energy.

Energy is another way of saying change. Energy causes change, and change is the result of the movement of energy. So, if we say the universe is made of energy, we can also say the universe is constantly changing. And every single particle in the universe is also constantly changing.

There are some very fundamental concepts about energy to keep in mind that will help us understand life and humans as we proceed. Let's use a pool game as an analogy. Picture the pre-universe as a teeny, tiny rack of billiard balls sitting on an unending pool table of nothingness. The "balls" are an almost invisible collection of energy bits whose nature we still don't understand. Let's say you, playing the role of a pool shark, hit the "balls" with a sharp stab of energy. Now, I'm pretty sure no one said, "Break!" before the energy balls flew out in every direction, but nevertheless, the energy bits went flying just like billiard balls on the pool table at your local bar. Now, if you play pool like I do, at least a few went flying over the edge of the table, but since the universe has no edge, this didn't happen. But it is true that the energy bits flew outward at different speeds and in different directions. Now remember, these "universe billiard balls" are not made of phenolic resin like earthly billiard balls. They are made of energy, and energy is very flexible. By moving at different speeds and directions, they changed rapidly.

Here's the important point: change in the universe does not act uniformly. That is, movement and change produce variation. So, they didn't all change in the same way. Some energy bits escaped so fast, they found themselves alone and unable to smash into other energy bits. Some of these became the force particles we know today. But some energy bits, in their haste to move, crashed into each other. These collisions produced many different forms: dark energy, which makes up 70% of our universe; dark matter, which makes up 24% of the universe; and visible matter, which makes up 6% of the universe. Yep, that's right, you and I are in the 6% group.

Because the conditions that existed when these collisions occurred were all slightly different, the complex energy forms that resulted were also different. Variation in the universe is as ubiquitous as change. Keep this concept in mind. We'll see it again.

I want to take a moment and return to our concentric circles. Scientists don't know much about dark energy and dark matter. Since we are part of the 6% group, it has been difficult to understand these parts of the universe that can only be inferred from mathematical calculations about how they affect visible matter. Scientists have not been able to actually observe these mysterious parts of the universe, much less understand their characteristics. So, it is difficult to understand their formation. Our concentric circle model would look likes this if all three types of materials were formed at once.

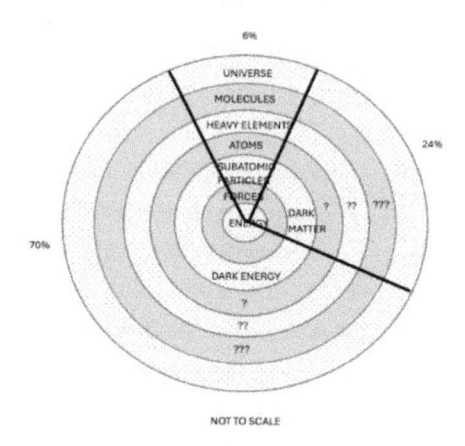

NOT TO SCALE

To me, this formation does not seem likely. From what we see on Earth, change does not produce radically different units all at once. Change flows step by step. To me, the universe seems more likely to have formed like this:

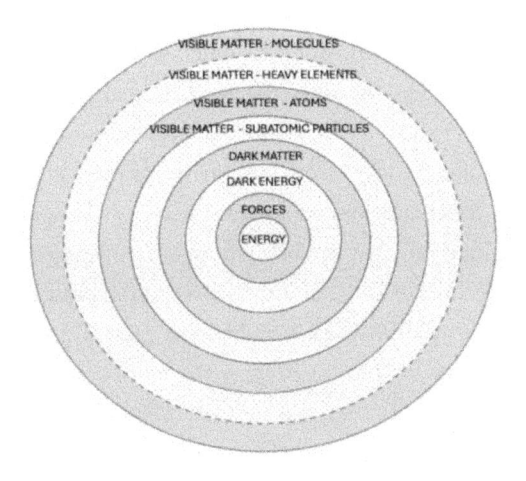

```
VISIBLE MATTER - MOLECULES
VISIBLE MATTER - HEAVY ELEMENTS
VISIBLE MATTER - ATOMS
VISIBLE MATTER - SUBATOMIC PARTICLES
DARK MATTER
DARK ENERGY
FORCES
ENERGY
```

This is just supposition, on my part. I use this image to illustrate how visible matter could logically be such a small part of the universe. Throughout the universe, complicated things always occur less frequently than simpler ones. Remember 92% of all visible matter is simple hydrogen and only 2% of all elements are larger than helium. Even on Earth, single celled organisms vastly outnumber multicellular animals. This arrangement would also explain why we, as members of the 6% group, cannot understand those energy units that preceded us. We don't share enough characteristics to be able to observe them.

Okay, back to our pool game. As you can see, our universe billiard balls did not remain as simple energy bits. Just as billiard balls slow down after the initial break, so did our energy bits. But unlike billiard balls, which just crash into each other and bounce off again, some energy bits were slowing down too much to boomerang away. They ended up sticking together. With time, these larger units began to collide and stick together with other bits to make even larger units. As the universe aged, it cooled, which means fewer things were able to break apart after a collision. This is why change looks like it moves from simple to complex. But that is not exactly true. It depends on the amount of energy hanging around. If there is a lot of energy, the bits will just fly into each other and bounce off again. But if the energy is dissipating with time, larger forms can emerge and remain and become even larger. The star is a perfect example of this. As long as there are enough hydrogen atoms hanging around, they will smoosh together to produce light and helium. Helium, in turn, will smoosh to form beryllium, an atom with four protons and four neutrons. And so on, until iron is formed. Iron is a pig. When iron is formed, instead of releasing energy, like all the elements before it, it absorbs energy. Once iron is formed the outward pressure eases, so gravity is free to squeeze the star which then explodes as a supernova. I'm pretty sure this is *not* how the term "pig iron" came about, but nevertheless, I still think iron is a pig.

Let's say that when you broke your initial group of billiard balls, they immediately dissolved and transformed into a kaleidoscope of blue butterflies and flew away. That would be awesome but impossible, not only for you, pool shark, but also for the universe at the beginning of the Big Bang. All change in the universe occurs step by step. Energy may be powerful, but it can only ever really do one thing. It can move, and as it moves, it can bump into other energy particles. Simple components cannot make anything but slightly more complex units. Complex change takes time. The universe eventually did create a blue butterfly, but it took 13.7 billion years and many step-by-step changes. Change must go in order, like a stairstep. The energy in the universe can only produce a blue butterfly if it goes step by step and makes all the other parts it needs first, like atoms and molecules and cells and bodies.

All energy forms are created incrementally. When you think about it, it basically took the universe 13.7 billion years of step-by-step changes to make a blue butterfly and 13.8 billion years of step-by-step changes to create a human on one little planet in one corner of the universe. Energy is powerful, but slow.

All energy particles have particular characteristics that make them behave in a particular way. Over time, scientists have discovered these laws of energy. These laws apply without exception, at least as far as our current knowledge extends. Given specific conditions, matter and forces will always act in a specific way. Think again about our pool game. If you hit the ball at a certain angle, it will deflect at that same angle. Every time. If you're a really good pool player, you'll hit the ball at the proper angle, and the ball will deflect right into the pocket. If you're a lousy pool player like me, you hit the ball, look at the deflected angle, and say, "Hmm, I never was very good at geometry."

The characteristics of energy do not change over time, but as more complex forms are produced, it gets harder to discern the individual laws at work because so many changed parts are jumbled together. Imagine all ten billiard balls glommed together in one irregularly shaped unit. The rule about angular momentum still exists, but now it's working on a clump of balls that slightly interact with each other, making it much more challenging to determine how that unit will move. Imagine how difficult these laws are to discern when we talk about humans' 13.8 billion years of evolutionary change all piled on top of each other.

Ironically, for all the specific laws that energy obeys, change in the universe is unpredictable. At each stairstep of change, matter and forces interact with each other. Multitudes of forms result, but only a few are stable enough to become the basis for further changes. Which ones? Your guess is as good as mine. Existence is contingent on an ever-expanding set of variables in an increasingly complex universe.

Think of it this way. If we consider a human that exists today, we can look backward and determine the changes that occurred from the beginning of time to produce this human. Energy. Atoms. Molecules. Cells. Multicellular entities. Humans. When history is laid out like this, it makes perfect sense that humans formed. We can follow the steps backward, one by one. But if we start at the beginning of the universe and look forward, it would be impossible to predict that humans would ever form. Too many variables can occur along the way for any prediction to be meaningful.

So, this is great. We have a universe made of one thing, energy, that can only do one thing, move, and it has just been hanging around for 13.8 billion years performing its one simple function. So, how the heck can we figure out how it all works?

Keys to Unlocking the Ideasphere:

- The universe is made entirely of energy that has evolved into different forms.
- The only thing energy can do is move. All energy forms are constantly moving, which means they are all constantly changing and producing a variety of shapes and structures.
- Matter is a particularly stable form of energy.
- Change occurs step by step. Simple energy forms crash into others and either fly apart or remain stuck together. The stuck-together units can collide into other energy forms and make even larger energy units.
- Change is slow. It took a long time to produce complicated life forms.
- Change adheres to particular rules, but because so many energy particles of varying sizes are constantly moving, the results of change become increasingly unpredictable.

Chapter 2

Environment

Energy creates environments. All things exist in environments. So, what's an environment? Good question. The environment is one of the strongest things we cannot see. Which makes it challenging to explain. Because we are talking about the universe, we can take a shortcut and say that environments are composed of energy. This is true, but that insight is not particularly helpful.

Let's define an environment as the combination of all energy particles in a given area that act in the only way they can, but together create certain overall conditions. The combined effect of the whole energy group, in turn, impacts each individual energy particle in the environment.

Let's use an analogy to describe an environment. Imagine you're having coffee at a café. We can think of the café as an environment. It is a specific location where energy exists. Some of the "energy particles" in the café environment are the building, the lights, the coffee, the staff, and the customers.

The café environment is constantly changing. Customers come and go. That's equivalent to energy entering and leaving an environment. The barista makes a vanilla latte. That is equivalent to energy particles bumping into each other and creating a new unit. Sometimes the aroma of coffee fills the air, and sometimes the smell of a fresh batch of almond croissants dominates. That is equivalent to energy particles just moseying around in the environment, just doing what they do. From moment to moment, the energy units in the café are constantly moving.

Each part of the café environment both affects and is affected by all the other parts. When you inhale the scent of the almond croissant, you realize you are hungry. A customer picks a seat by the window where the sun is shining so they can enjoy the warmth. Another customer bites into a blueberry muffin. But even in a simple environment like our café, every component acts differently based on how the other components interact with them. Some components, like the building and equipment, don't change much at all. But some components change frequently, like the customers who drop in, or the cups that are used to deliver lattes, or the selection of bakery items in the display case near the counter. The more variables in an environment, the greater the number of possible outcomes that can result from their interactions. It doesn't take long for our simple café to become a stunningly complex environment.

The more complex the environment, the more unpredictable the results of the interactions within it will be. Let's return to you and your vanilla latte. It seems like a simple scene, but actually, the café environment is insidiously working to change you. The latte you are drinking travels to your stomach, where it is broken down into energy and nutrients to fuel every cell in your body. The mystery novel you're reading while you sip your drink affects your brain and memory. The aroma of the freshly baked cinnamon rolls that were just put into the display case brings back memories from your childhood. All these things may work together to put you in a good mood this morning. Do you see how complicated an environment can get? And this is just a simple illustration of a made-up moment in a fictional café in a not-so-make-believe book. Environments are complicated and unpredictable. Direct lines between cause and effect are often difficult to discern in environments because so many energy events are happening simultaneously.

Let's continue with our café analogy. Let's say a large rock suddenly flies through the window and hits the customer at the next table in the head, knocking him unconscious. Things like this happen in environments. Unexpected energy events can occur at any time, and once they do, they affect everything that happens afterward. Actually, every change affects everything that happens afterward, but many effects are so small they go unnoticed. The unexpected ones, however, can really stand out. Once a change occurs, it cannot be undone. Our rock victim is forever altered by this event. He may die. He may suffer a brain injury. Or he may recover and regain his previous capabilities. But he forever goes forward with the experience of being hit by the rock at the café. Changes in an environment affect the things inside—sometimes significantly, sometimes insignificantly, but always irrevocably.

Environments cannot be neatly cataloged with precise boundaries. The boundaries may be tight, but they are not impermeable. Our coffee shop has doors that are unlocked during the day, allowing other energy units, I mean customers, to enter. At night, those doors are locked to prevent those very same customers from coming in. But even at night, energy enters and leaves the café. Deliveries may be made in the back. The cool night air pulls heat from inside the café out through the closed windows. The alarm system detects movement outside and records the information on a computer in the back office. A café is a much tighter environment than our universe. In the universe, energy just moves wherever it can. Energy in the universe doesn't respect boundaries.

Environments are important because they are way stations for relatively consistent changes. Our café is a way station for trading beverages and bakery items for money. Of course, a lot of other things happen in our café environment, but this is one major thing that happens consistently. We can think of the early universe as a way station for making hydrogen atoms.

Environments have relatively loose boundaries, so energy constantly flows into and out of them; they are always changing. At the same time, they are stable enough to enable the forms inside to interact and even combine to create more energy forms. You're probably tired of our café analogy by now, but let's go back for one more latte. Let's say a customer comes in and orders a half-caf blond roast oat milk latte with a shot of toffee nut flavoring topped with whipped cream. Our customer has caused a lot more energy to be expended on this order as opposed to the previous customer who ordered "Coffee. Black." The staff can make this complicated drink because they have all the components for it in the café. To get complex forms in the universe, simpler forms need to be present and capable of sticking around long enough to interact with other forms. An environment is a stable enough place to produce such changes.

The earth is an environment. It has a clear boundary, yet energy floods into and out of the earth every moment of every day, primarily from the sun. Since its formation 4.5 billion years ago, Earth has undergone some wild changes, but it has been stable enough to produce matter that evolved into simple life forms that further evolved into complex life forms. Let's take a quick peek at Earth's history.

Earth was extremely hot and looked like a molten bowling ball when it first formed. Early in Earth's history, it's theorized that a planet named Theia crashed into Earth, tilted the planet by 23 degrees, and blew so much material into space that it formed the moon that still rotates around the "combo planet." Theia merged into Earth and, in doing so, deposited a lot of iron into Earth's core, giving the conjoined planet an extra-strong magnetic field. We will never know if and what energy forms might have developed on the "pre-Theia Earth." That environment was destroyed when the collision occurred. Every new form that emerged after the crash needed to comply with the new conditions that resulted from the impact. The tilt of the earth caused seasons, the moon caused tides, and the strong magnetic fields prevented excess solar radiation from hitting the earth's surface. The life forms that exist today all survive because they conform to these post-collision conditions.

As Earth's surface cooled, its core and mantle remained extraordinarily hot, as they do even today. When molten material found a weak point in the earth's crust, it would force its way to the surface, form a volcano, and spew out hot material all over the cooling surface. The intense heat from these explosions could break apart molecules or smoosh them together. We know what happens when energy forms collide at high speeds—they either join together, blow apart, or end up in some combination of the two. This is the very same process that occurs throughout the universe, but on Earth, the energy levels are a bit lower than those in a star. Volcanic action was instrumental in pushing gases that were trapped inside the earth out to form the atmosphere and, as the planet continued to cool, the oceans.

At first, the combination of matter and water and energy produced new and different forms of matter. But just as the energy particles of the new universe created matter that could do things that energy could not, Earth's matter created a new energy form that could do something that matter could not. That proved to be a game-changer.

Keys to Understanding the Ideasphere:
- An environment is a collection of energy particles in a given area that create certain overall conditions.
- Energy is constantly moving, so environments are constantly changing.
- The forms within an environment affect each other and, in turn, affect the nature of the environment.
- Energy moves into and out of environments, which irrevocably affects the forms inside.
- Change within an environment can be relatively stable.
- Earth is an environment.

Chapter 3

Life

How did life form? We cannot know the answer with absolute certainty because we cannot recreate every possible condition in the precise sequence starting from the time Earth was formed to prove exactly how life emerged. Early Earth didn't leave us many clues; however, scientists have mapped out everything they do know about the conditions of early Earth and have concluded that it was possible for life to form along a variety of paths.

In the last chapter, we left our early Earth with a newly formed atmosphere and vast oceans.

Water is cool, not only with respect to temperature but also because of the wide variety of things it can do. Water can dissolve many forms of matter into their component parts. Given that matter particles are just squirmy little energy bits, those component parts can then join together to make other pieces of matter. Does this sound familiar? That is how energy particles have been behaving since the universe began. The difference is that these energy forms are much more complex than those hydrogen atoms hanging out in the core of a star. And a scooch cooler.

We can't say exactly how life formed, but we can surmise that certain events occurred in a specific order. The earth formed about 4.5 billion years ago, which means the universe was already 9.3 billion years old if you're up to doing the math. The simple elements and compounds that landed on Earth from asteroids and comets and meteorites, plus the ones that formed in oceans, started mixing it up.

Four types of important matter emerged in Earth's early years. The first are **lipids**, or fats. These molecules cannot dissolve in water. They usually exist as spheres because that's the best shape for equalizing pressure from surrounding water. **Carbohydrates** are relatively simple molecules made of carbon, hydrogen, and oxygen that form long strings and contain a lot of energy in the bonds that hold them together. **Amino acids** are molecules that can form long strings, which we call proteins. Proteins are impressive. Depending on their components and shape, proteins can perform a multitude of actions, from starting chemical reactions to forming structures with unique capabilities. Your body is loaded with proteins, from your toenails, your bones, and your blood, to the hairs on your head. **Nucleic acids** are complex nitrogen-based molecules hooked together in long strings. Scientists think many types of nucleic acids existed in Earth's early years, but today only two exist: ribonucleic acid and deoxyribonucleic acid, or as we call them, RNA and DNA.

Okay, our table is set. Let's see what happened. As soon as the earth was cool enough, these types of matter—lipids, carbohydrates, amino acids, and nucleic acids—began to populate the oceans in large numbers. And what do energy bits do when they find themselves in the same environment? They move around and run into each other. You can imagine it was pretty much a free-for-all. Lipids and carbohydrates and amino acids and nucleic acids all swimming free in a big ocean, running into each other willy-nilly. Every combination that could be tried was tried. Just like in the early universe. But just as in the early universe, only combined forms that were stable in the environment lasted. We can assume that most combinations didn't make it past the first interaction, but some did.

About 750 million years into the free-for-all, a particular combination emerged that had staying power. Let's take a closer look at this weirdo energy combo.

This thing was round because it had an outer shell made of lipids. The shell repelled water on the outside but contained water on the inside too. A few proteins among the vast array of proteins swimming around had the ability to collide with the lipid shell and open it up to allow water inside before the shell could close up again. The water carried our four matter particles with it as it entered the shell. Once inside, the lipids and carbohydrates and amino acids and nucleic acids began to interact once more. Essentially, the lipid shell created an environment for whatever managed to squirm inside. What happens when energy forms find themselves in a stable environment? They crash into each other and make new forms.

And that's what happened.

The real problem child inside the shell was RNA. DNA and RNA are related, but they couldn't be more different. RNA contains ribose sugar, and DNA contains deoxyribose sugar, which is just a fancy way of saying it has one less oxygen atom. The extra oxygen atom in

RNA made all the difference—it made RNA super reactive. DNA, on the other hand, was stable as a rock. RNA could react with anything. When RNA bumped into carbohydrates, it would break their bonds and release energy. When it bumped into amino acids, the amino acids would react by forming long protein strings. But a really interesting thing happened when RNA ran into super-stable DNA.

RNA was like a pesky little brother who wants to play with the big kids. RNA would bump into DNA over and over and over. And every once in a while, RNA would get under DNA's skin, and DNA would freak out. This is not a precise scientific description, but you get the idea. If RNA had enough energy to hit the DNA particularly hard, DNA would literally unravel into two parts. The two halves of the DNA string, preferring to be stable, would immediately seek out the parts needed to regain their original stable structure. This resulted in two strings of DNA where there had been only one before. Essentially, DNA, with RNA's help, could copy itself. RNA could copy itself too, but it took a few extra steps. And because RNA was so reactive, it could get distracted in the process and end up making something else instead.

So, all this stuff is going on inside our lipid shell with RNA accelerating the action. If the shell grew too big from all these changes, it would stretch until it broke apart. Sometimes, that was the end of our little unit, but sometimes, the shells managed to reform into smaller units that contained enough material to continue the change process.

There were likely billions and billions of different versions of these units running around with varying levels of longevity. Sometimes, a protein would open the lipid shell but couldn't close it before water flooded the whole shell and blew it apart. Or RNA busted so many carbohydrates at once that the shell exploded from too much energy. Or RNA created proteins that penetrated the inside of the shell and blew it apart. But with all the failures, successes occurred too. Sometimes, reactions enabled the unit to last and become the basis for even more interactions.

If you want to know how RNA and DNA interact in more detail, I have included a more in-depth explanation in Appendix 1. You don't have to remember any of the particulars of this process, but what I want to emphasize is that all the particles on early Earth swam around in the earth's oceans, colliding, sticking together, and coming apart as the ocean environment allowed. This behavior is exactly the same as all the other energy particles in the universe.

Now, back to our weirdo successful energy combo. Our spherical lipid is filled with water but can repel water on the outside. Proteins inside bump into the inner shell and temporarily wedge open the outer shell to allow water inside. The water entering the lipid is filled with a healthy mix of our four molecules. Once the molecules are trapped inside, RNA starts reacting, creating energy and other types of proteins. When these reactions produce materials the unit does not need, some proteins bump into the inner rim of the lipid, open an exit, and usher those useless particles outside. Occasionally, the RNA collides with a DNA strand and copies it. When the lipid unit expands to a size where the shell can no longer hold all the materials inside, it breaks apart and re-forms into two new, smaller units filled with the same materials that go on to repeat these same actions.

It took a long, long time for the units to develop this sequence of actions to happen the same way every time. But once they did, there was no stopping them. Think about it. They had all the bases covered. They were encased in a protected environment. They could obtain resources when they needed them. They could produce both the proteins the unit needed to operate as well as the energy to produce those proteins. And they could make an identical copy of themselves when they grew too big. It was such a winning combination that none of the other wannabe units running around could match their abilities.

Why is this important? These successful little units aren't really weirdos. They are what we call cells. And all the activities happening inside the cell? That is what we call "life."

> Keys to Unlocking the Ideasphere:
> - The basic life unit is a cell.
> - A cell is composed entirely of nonliving matter.
> - The nonliving matter in the cell work together to make the cell alive.
> - To be alive, a cell must be protected from the outside environment, obtain resources, turn the resources into energy and food, and copy itself.
> - RNA and DNA are critical for a cell to be able to survive and replicate itself.

PART 2

ECOSYSTEM 1

DNA and the Cell

Chapter 4

The Characteristics of Life

Life. What is life? It may be an existential question, but it's also a practical one. To be life, a cell must do three things:

- It must be protected from the outside environment. Thank you, lipids.
- It must be able to acquire and consume resources. Thank you, carbohydrates and proteins.
- It must be able to copy itself. Thank you, RNA and DNA.

All the particles found in our early oceans combined to create this thing we call life. When you think about all the attempts it must have taken for this model to emerge and endure, I'm surprised it took only 750 million years.

Those first cells were a huge demarcation event in the history of the universe. Before this, energy particles could only join together or break apart. But life did something that had never been accomplished before. The bits of matter inside those cells, by working together, were able to transform the materials they consumed into new cell parts. Further, by copying themselves, they could transfer this ability to a brand-new cell. This is something the brightest stars cannot do.

So, let's look at life in more detail. Understanding living things is essential. Humans physically operate the same way every other life form does, but because of the human idea, the results that humans produce are radically different. So, if we want to really understand humans, we must first understand how we would work without ideas, which, of course, is how every other living entity on earth operates.

First, a timeline. We call the first cells that emerged 3.8 billion years ago prokaryotes (pronounced: "pro carry oats"). These little guys had a hard outside shell and a mishmash of proteins, carbohydrates, RNA, and DNA inside. Like every life form before and after, prokaryotes constantly evolved. About two billion years ago, very organized one-cell organisms emerged from the prokaryote group that were so much more efficient they were given a separate name. These guys are called eukaryotes (pronounced: "you carry oats"). Eukaryotes were so adept at survival that they pushed prokaryotes into secluded nooks and crannies and basically took over the rest of the world. Eukaryotes also constantly evolved. About 600 million years ago, eukaryotes evolved a line of multicelled entities. About 450 million years ago, multicellular plants that grew on land emerged. About 200,000 years ago, sapiens emerged, and Homo sapiens emerged from this group. So, if we look at the big picture, we are merely a tiny moment in Earth's vast history.

Now, let's look at some important details of life so we can understand how utterly different life is from the matter from which it came.

Building Blocks

The dance between RNA and DNA is the key element that makes life operate the way it does. They are the linchpin of life. The RNA-DNA team was pretty much unstoppable from the get-go. And still is. Because DNA is so stable, it can store long strings that, when activated, provide instructions the cell needs to operate. By instructions, I mean that DNA directs RNA to produce a particular protein, stop producing a particular protein, or make a DNA copy when RNA hits the DNA. DNA instructions are always safe and protected in the nucleus. But DNA cannot initiate action or copy itself, so it needs RNA to start the process.

Over time, the RNA-DNA team became tightly linked. The cells that limited RNA to only following DNA's instructions fared better than the ones in which RNA reacted every which way it could. Over time, those cells with the successful "DNA as director" team dominated. Today, every multicellular creature uses the RNA-DNA team model, where DNA provides the instructions and RNA merely carries them out. All of us, humans included, have evolved from that successful arrangement. We share 32% of our DNA with yeast, 70% with fish, and 99% with other primates. In essence, we are all members of one giant family.

DNA is the most successful material on Earth. It has housed itself in a myriad of forms that have survived for several billion years and burrowed into every corner of this planet. Yet DNA is indifferent to the forms it takes. It does not matter to DNA which entities survive, as long as some do. To DNA, a yeast particle is just as valuable as a fish or a human. If we look at life this way and are willing to be a bit humbled in the process, we can see that it is DNA that rules the earth, not humans.

Fit

Let's talk survival. Survival is the process of converting resources into the specific nutrients that an entity needs to live. If our creature lives long enough to produce and rear offspring, it will have successfully transferred its previously consumed resources into a new generation.

All beings strive to survive. What is the primary determinant of who survives and who doesn't? The great unseen power—the environment. For an entity to survive, it must fit into its environment. If a change occurs that endangers its ability to survive, it must adapt to that change or risk death. In their effort to survive, creatures can adapt by moving to a more hospitable location, changing the resources they consume, or even producing more offspring with slight variations.

Producing offspring was a particularly successful survival technique. If an entity produced more offspring, more of them might survive a dangerous event. But there is another critical reason why procreation was important. Remember change? It's everywhere. Every time the RNA-DNA team created a protein or made a copy of DNA, a change occurred. An opportunity for change is also an opportunity for an unexpected outcome, or variation. Unexpected outcomes are not mistakes; nature does not make mistakes. These unexpected outcomes are merely logical results of a changing environment or an unpredictable energy event. When offspring contain slightly different DNA, they also exhibit slightly different characteristics. The differences may be minor, but when an environment undergoes dramatic change, even minute variations might make the difference between life and death.

Charles Darwin called this process "descent by modification." He first proposed it in *The Origin of Species* in 1859. Darwin hypothesized that each generation changes, or evolves, based on the impact the environment has on existing life forms. He used the term "natural selection" to explain how entities with characteristics most suitable to the environment would survive and those with less suitable characteristics would die out. The accumulation of many small changes over millions and billions of years gave rise to the different forms of life that exist today.

If we rolled back time and viewed Earth's history in 1,000-year increments, we would see entities emerging, surviving, and dying on an ever-changing planet. Scientists don't really know how many species have existed, but estimates range as high as six billion, and almost all of them are now extinct. The species living today represent a mere 1% of all the ones that have ever lived.

Here's the thing: Lots of animals have lived and died, but DNA has never died. True, perhaps only 1% of all the DNA forms that ever existed are still alive today, but those numbers obscure the real point. DNA is still plugging along. If we do the math, at least 60 million species exist today. To put it another way, 60 million different DNA versions are running around in the current Earth environment. If we consider it this way, DNA is pretty darn successful. Humans? We represent 1/60,000,000th of all the species that exist today. Enough said.

Life can be defined as one long, single flow of DNA continuously repackaged into different forms. The forms don't die as much as they alter their structure to match their environment as each new generation emerges. If we view life from the perspective of DNA, nothing has ever gone extinct. Humans and all the plants and animals alive today are merely the current set of DNA containers that best fit the present planetary conditions. Our bodies are made up of more than 35 trillion cells and nothing else, and every one of our cells contains DNA. We are not humans with DNA; we are a collaboration of DNA cells made into human form.

Death

Every living entity eventually dies. Without fail. With life comes death. Why do you think this is?

First, let's define death. Energy is embedded in every single particle of matter on this earth. The particles inside an atom constantly move; the atoms inside a molecule constantly move; the molecules inside a cell constantly move. Energy in the form of nutrients and proteins constantly moves to nourish a body. If the energy within a body stops moving for a long enough time, the cells stop functioning. That is death.

Death can occur due to external forces. For example, a large rock can fall on my head and crush my skull. Ouch. If my brain can no longer direct the functions of my body, I'll die, or more precisely, all my cells will die.

Or I can die from a malfunction. My heart may become obstructed and stop pumping, thus impeding the flow of blood through my circulatory system, once again killing all my cells. . . and me. We call this type of external cell death necrosis. A cell dying by necrosis releases its contents into the body in a disorderly manner. This can endanger nearby cells, resulting in inflammation, which can kill more cells and even the entire body.

In certain circumstances, if a cell in a body encounters negative stimuli, it will commit suicide. We call this process apoptosis. Exposure to hazardous chemicals, immune reactions, infectious agents, and even high temperatures or radiation may cause cell damage that leads to cell suicide. In this case, the cell will shrink and then be eaten by phagocytes, which are small cells whose job is to absorb a dying cell's material before its contents can be released into the body. Apoptosis is a natural process. It starts early and continues throughout the lifetime of all living entities.

Apoptosis exists because it worked better than all the other survival methods early life forms tried. If an entity could remove injured cells *and* use their parts as resources for the remaining cells, it would have a much better shot at surviving than those without that capability. As long as most cells survive at any one time, the body won't die from losing a few cells.

The cells of an entity work together to keep the entity alive. The cell's ability to kill itself is a survival strategy designed to keep most cells and the entity alive. To be more precise, the DNA within the cell instructs itself to die if the condition of the cell will endanger the survival of the entity. As long as some cells survive, DNA survives; that's what's important.

Just as DNA adheres to strict timing and protocols to enable new offspring to be born and develop into adults, it also has mechanisms in place to allow them to die if they do not succumb to accidents or illness.

Inside the nucleus, the DNA is wrapped with proteins in tight bundles called chromosomes. At the end of each chromosome is a protein called a telomere. The telomere is a long string with many little sections, like beads on a string. Its job is to keep the chromosome geometrically stable. Every time a DNA cell replicates, every bit of the chromosome is copied except the last bead of the telomere string. This process repeats each time the cell undergoes replication, and each time, another bead of the telomere chain is lopped off. When no telomeres are left, the cell can no longer replicate. If a negative stimulus then hits the cell, damage may result. It may die, or it may commit suicide. If enough cells in the body die this way, the body dies. This is how an entity dies from old age. Sooner or later, constantly moving energy in the form of deadly stimuli catches up to enough cells, and the entity dies.

Why does it work this way? Why didn't DNA develop a more efficient process that copied the entire telomere and allowed the cell to live forever? Good question. It tried. It just didn't work.

Telomeres serve as the stop sign for replication. Once the enzyme reaches the telomere, it stops copying and unhooks from the gene. The telomeres evolved to make sure the entire chromosome remained stable while the process occurred. However, like RNA, telomeres are highly reactive. The longer the telomere string is, the more likely it is to react uncontrollably. This can result in illnesses like cancer. If the string is too short, the beads may run out before the entity can produce offspring. A balance evolved—short enough to prevent uncontrollable copying but long enough to allow the entity time to procreate. So, entities with either longer or shorter telomere strings tended to die out before they could procreate. Only the string lengths enabling the occurrence of both events—long enough to procreate but short enough to prevent unwanted copying—survived. The telomere strings that exist in each entity today are balanced not because they are perfect but because they survived. Part of the legacy that each entity inherits is an imperfect, yet adequate, telomere length. Human telomeres last until we're about 55 years old. Of course, this varies with each individual, but generally sometime after age 55, our cells stop replicating and become subject to the energy forces around us.

The human body, like all living bodies, is a mechanism for DNA to store itself. From the DNA perspective, as long as humans can pass their DNA on to a new generation, DNA's survival is ensured. Over time, the DNA entities that created new generations of entities with fresh, new telomere strings survived more easily than the entities with longer telomere strings. DNA's ability to pass a version of itself on to the next generation of bodies ended up being the most efficient method for its survival. The death of the older entity is not important if a new entity with new DNA now exists. So, ironically, we can think of death as a survival strategy. Not for humans. For DNA.

Risk

Living is a risky undertaking. Given that the environment is enormous and constantly changing, danger can lurk around every corner. Fires and floods can happen, resources can disappear, meteors can strike. Living entities can die at any moment. The reality of life is that we are constantly at risk of dying.

Matter doesn't die. Because it doesn't ingest resources, convert them into another form, or procreate, it is not a living thing. It's just stuff. It is only when stuff turned into life that death became a thing. Dying is the cost of living.

Resources

Resources are the raw materials a creature consumes to survive. All entities need two types of resources to survive. Proteins and minerals are needed to build and maintain cells. Carbohydrates are needed to provide energy to fuel the cell-building processes. To operate optimally, all bodies must consume a balance between the two.

When you eat a spinach salad, your body breaks it down and converts it into proteins that nourish your cells. In essence, your body converted the spinach into a slightly different human body.

Matter does not work like this. When hydrogen atoms join, they become a helium atom and release excess energy into the environment. This process produces a different element with different characteristics. But the components themselves do not change. If you hit the helium atom with enough energy, it would split back into two hydrogen atoms. If you split our spinach-eating human apart, we could not pull the spinach out of them intact, no matter how hard we tried. This is a fundamental difference between life and matter. Living entities consume materials and absorb them into their bodies in a process that can't be reversed.

Each time a body goes through this conversion process, it shifts the balance of resources in the environment. If all entities consume resources, make larger versions of themselves, and convert their resources into offspring, the mix of resources in the environment irrevocably changes.

Environments containing life change faster than environments made only of matter, mainly because it takes a lot less energy to make a new cell on Earth than to make a new element in space.

Complexity

Living things evolve from simple to complex, just like the energy in the universe. Complexity takes time. It's interesting that it took only 750 million years for a single-celled prokaryote to form, but it took 1.8 billion years for our disorganized one-celled prokaryote to evolve into an organized one-celled eukaryote. It took another billion years for one-celled eukaryotes to evolve into multicelled creatures.

Movement towards complexity is slow and not particularly efficient. Energy forms experiment with every conceivable combination along their journey. Unsuccessful attempts far outnumber the occasional successes. Each successful change must proceed step-by-step as it evolves.

Most cells are microscopic, so it doesn't take much energy to affect them. An unusual fluctuation in temperature or contact with natural radiation may be enough to alter the DNA of a one-celled creature. If an alteration causes a cell to survive more easily than its unchanged neighbors, it will likely proliferate and may crowd the others out of existence. If a change makes it more difficult to survive, then the cell may die, leaving the unchanged survivors to proliferate instead. A modification to a gene here, a mutation caused by radiation there— it takes many years for small changes to accumulate and produce creatures with different shapes and structures.

On the surface, it seems that complex entities should never have evolved at all. Because complex forms are bigger, they need more energy to live. Wouldn't that be a disadvantage in an environment where everyone needs resources? Yet complex entities thrive on Earth. Cells existing in multicelled entities represent over 80% of all life. How can this be if complex life forms had an evolutionary disadvantage? Trick question. It wasn't a disadvantage at all.

Complexity is another term for organization. Life began the way all things begin: simple. Prokaryotes were a jumble of the components of life swirled together inside the cell. Eukaryotes, on the other hand, were much more efficient. They were loaded with organelles—little sub-environments—each performing a function that the cell needed to survive and copy itself. Though eukaryotes were much larger than their prokaryote forerunners, they could function more efficiently, that is, do more with fewer resources.

Efficiency is the important concept here. Any cell that can survive with fewer resources or produce more offspring with the same resources stands a better chance of living in an uncertain environment. Organization is simply the process of breaking down jobs into progressively smaller components so they can be done more efficiently. Increased organization inevitably leads to greater complexity.

Prokaryotes never grew organized enough to create efficient multicelled organisms. They still exist all over this earth as single or, at most, dual-celled creatures. Eukaryotes? They have evolved into all sorts of complex forms and now exist in every corner of this earth.

Every time an entity changes, the change must allow the entire body to function, or the entity will not survive. As creatures become more complex, changes are more difficult to achieve, and fewer of them result. The actual numbers reflect this reality. Far fewer complex forms exist, whether we are speaking about elements of matter or living entities. When a complex living entity does become successful, it has the potential to dominate others and alter the entire panorama of life. I'm looking at you, humans!

Self-Interest

Over the years, much has been written about how all animals in the ecosystem act in their self-interest, so humans should be free to do so as well, regardless of the consequences to their fellow humans. Fair warning: I don't buy into this concept.

Let's start by determining why creatures act in their self-interest. In nature, all life forms strive to survive. They do whatever they must to survive, including killing and eating other entities. But that's not the whole story. Living beings can survive in a variety of ways. Consider how the bee draws nectar from a flower and, in so doing, carries pollen to other flowers. This is a mutually beneficial relationship. The bees obtain resources, and the flower procreates. No killing anywhere in sight.

Life forms, at least nonhuman life forms, act without intention. They do whatever it takes to survive given the environment in which they live. Remember the DNA-RNA team? This team creates and carries out the instructions to enable a creature to live. A creature can only do what its DNA instructs it to do. And how does DNA know what to do? Lots and lots of years of evolution.

Let's say the DNA inside a creature has long instructed it to produce a specific protein that has enabled this creature to survive. Suddenly, the environment changes, and this protein that had previously been so beneficial now proves to be deadly in the new environment. The creature can't change the instruction. It's stuck in the new environment with its old rules. Its chances of survival are now reduced.

All nonhuman life is reactive. It can only do what it is programmed to do and no more. There is no intent, and consequently, there is no self-interest. What we perceive as self-interest is merely the result of successful survival instructions lodged inside the DNA of every creature that was inherited from a long line of successfully surviving ancestors.

Order

Picture the earth as a wheel. Inside the wheel, every square inch of the planet is covered with a host of entities that have survived through multiple generations and are all compatible with the environment. Each entity survives the same way: they consume resources, convert them to nutrients and energy, procreate, and die. When they die, their bodies break down and are consumed by other entities. Every single life form is both prey and predator. This process occurs over and over and over.

Each turn of the wheel produces a slightly different mix of entities. If, by chance, the environment goes through a massive change, many entities may die. The mix of entities is changed, but the wheel of life continues as if nothing happened.

If we stumbled upon this planet 200,000 years ago, it would look as if all entities were designed to fit on the earth. Which, in fact, they were. They have been designed by the environment and eons and eons of DNA replication.

The earth appears orderly from a distance. On closer examination, we find each entity inside the wheel trying to survive as its DNA instructions allow. Nonhuman entities do not possess any tools to help them; their bodies are their only tools. They are constantly on the move to procure resources while avoiding becoming resources themselves. Though the wheel of life appears stable from the outside, from the inside, it is a constantly moving, ever-changing network of resource-seeking beings striving to survive.

The order you see is an illusion. Down at the bottom, where the real living is done, chaos rules. So, how did any creature ever manage to survive in this mess?

Keys to Unlocking the Ideasphere:
- Life is an energy form that works differently than all previous energy forms. It consumes resources and turns them into a larger body or, in some cases, an entirely new entity.
- Over time, single cells evolved into the multicelled life forms we see today. All life forms are composed of individual cells.
- The major differences between matter and life:
    o RNA and DNA hold and process information in the nucleus of a cell so the cell can survive. They are the essential building blocks from which life is built. RNA and DNA that exist independently outside of a cell are matter and are not alive.
    o All living entities must fit the conditions of their environment to survive.
    o Death is a mechanism to ensure that new cells with new DNA maximize their chance of survival.
    o With life comes the risk of death.
    o All living entities must consume resources to obtain the energy and proteins required to keep their bodies working. Without resources, a living entity will die.
    o Complex living entities evolve when their components become more organized and more efficient in using resources.

- All animals strive to survive. The DNA in a cell is a set of survival instructions. Animals follow these directions. The instructions require an animal to do whatever it can to survive, so self-interest, to the extent it exists, is an instruction, not an intentional action.
- The earth is a chaotic, ever-changing environment.

Chapter 5

Competition

The earth is a system that harbors life. We call it the ecosystem. In the ecosystem, all entities must consume resources to survive. When living entities vie for the same resources, they compete. Competition was the first survival mechanism to exist, and it still exists today.

Competition occurs at every level of life—from the one-celled organism competing for nutrients in a pond, to large elephants eating only plants, to cheetahs eating other animals—every single living being vies for the resources it needs to survive.

There are other survival mechanisms, but competition came first, and like all forerunners, it has staying power. Competition is beneficial, but it also has disadvantages. It's important to understand how and when it should be used, especially as it pertains to humans.

All living entities require space to live and food to survive. Consequently, most competition occurs between individual members of a species. These individuals consume the same resources and are typically found in the same physical areas. Cross-species competition also occurs, but less frequently. For example, leopards and servals both share a genetic disposition to hunt okapi, but more competition occurs between leopards and between servals than across the two species.

The hallmark of competition is pressure. Every waking moment of a competitor's life is stressful. The most common pressure is scarcity of resources. If resources are abundant, all entities can eat their fill and procreate without much difficulty. In this situation, there is little pressure. But if resources are scarce, competition intensifies, and those more capable of obtaining resources have a better chance of surviving than those who aren't.

Ironically, competitive success breeds not just more offspring but also more pressure. If a living entity is efficient at ingesting resources, it procreates more successfully. What happens when many individuals of the same species are good at procuring resources? Competition intensifies. Siblings or not, only those most skilled at obtaining resources will survive. If there are more competitors than food, the stronger siblings will weed out the weaker ones.

An abundance of predators also poses survival pressure. For obvious reasons. It's pretty hard to munch on resources when you yourself are being munched on.

Competition is brutal. Let's see why.

Accountability

Competition forces every creature to bear the consequences of its actions. It is a system of total accountability. If a creature is better at survival and it procreates, it still dies, but its descendants benefit from an improved chance of survival. If an entity gets eaten by a predator or starves to death before producing offspring, it not only dies, but it's further penalized by having no descendants. Its DNA vanishes forever. This is the very definition of accountability. Competition is a win-lose arrangement.

Diversity

Competition produces diversity. Every individual creature inherits a slightly different set of DNA from their parents. The pressures of competition work on each individual to separate the fit from the unfit. The fit survive, and the unfit die. Each fit survivor produces offspring with slightly different sets of DNA. Competition then winnows them down to only those with the best survival characteristics. Over time, creatures contain less similar DNA and look less alike. The more pressure there is in an environment, the faster this diversity process occurs.

Like all energy forms, life tries many variations. Every single variation is then tested by competition. An organism evolving a minor change still must compete in an environment in which all its competitors are the latest winners in life's contest. Most variations did not last, just as most versions of matter forming in the early universe did not last, or most versions of self-replicating one-celled organisms on early Earth did not last. But the few that did succeed proliferated because their variations strengthened their survival chances. This is how competition forced entities to diversify. Over time, they become new and different species, each with a different structure that fit their environment.

Innovation and Efficiency

Competition drives innovation and efficiency. If an entity changes in a way that allows it to survive more easily than its competitors, we can say the change is an improvement, or an innovation. Darwin found this when he studied the birds on the Galápagos Islands. A few finches found their way to the Galápagos Islands from the coast of South America. Over time, the finches evolved unique structures that enabled them to eat the plants that existed on their particular island. Each change to the birds' structure was an innovation that improved their chance of surviving. That is how innovation works. Over time, these innovations enabled them to better obtain resources in their particular environment. The innovations were then incorporated into subsequent generations. All life forms work this same way. Over time, the environment becomes populated with efficient entities that appear to be designed to live in their environment. Indeed, they are designed; by the environment itself.

Avoidance

Competition is hard. Creatures survived by successfully responding to the pressures surrounding them. Sometimes that meant avoiding competition altogether. Some creatures started eating different resources so they wouldn't have to struggle against so many competitors. Some just up and moved.

Like matter before life, and energy before matter, creatures only do what they can do. If survival is threatened and an entity can move, it will move. If it moves to a new environment where it finds food and doesn't face as much competition, its chances of survival increase. If a creature faces fewer competitive pressures, it will likely produce many offspring. Many offspring lead to many variations. As time goes on, the competitive pressure will build up and once again force creatures to search out new locations or resources. This is why entities are stuffed into every nook and cranny of this earth. They strive to find their own environmental niche with as few competitors as possible.

Sometimes, entities avoid direct competition by accessing different parts of the same resource. Birds fly during the day, and bats fly during the night in the same environment, thus not getting in each other's way. Some bees developed different lengths of proboscides so they could access nectar from different depths of the same flower.

Entities can also avoid competition by attacking or even killing their rivals. They perform this action most often when competing for mates, but it also happens when they're protecting their territory or taking over a competitor's territory. Infanticide is the most common form of intraspecies murder. It makes sense, really. If you want to dominate, destroy the rival's offspring so their DNA can't continue. Brutal, but effective.

Animals of the same species rarely fight over resources such as food or space. The risk of dying when attacking a rival of the same approximate size and strength is quite high, so most animals avoid competition by using other less risky techniques.

Even plants can take actions to avoid competition. Some trees emit poison, thus preventing their seeds or seeds from other trees from growing too close to the parent tree and crowding it out.

Despite all these effective methods of avoiding competition, competition still exists. The earth is finite. Its resources are finite. No matter how hard an organism tries to avoid competition, their reprieve is ever only temporary. Competition always returns. Reproductive success plants the seeds of competitive pressure. Producing many offspring forces the new generation to compete for resources. The more offspring, the higher the pressure. The pressure creates competition, and the competition creates not only diversity but also renewed efforts to find new resources or new environments. Competition drives life outward to more and more unpopulated areas. Over time, Earth becomes loaded with diverse, efficient organisms. Nevertheless, some life forms managed to figure out how to permanently avoid competition.

Those clever little guys. How do you think they did that?

Unlocking the Keys to the Ideasphere:
- Competition is the default survival mechanism for all living entities.
- Competition primarily occurs among individual members of a species who consume the same resources and are found in the same physical area.
- We can define competition as pressure. The more pressure there is, whether it's food or space or predators, the more intense the competition to survive will be.
- Competitive success leads to more offspring, which in turn leads to more competition.

- Animals respond by doing what they can to avoid competition. They move, eat different food, or try to live on fewer resources.
- Competition produces certain outcomes:
    o Accountability. An animal will either live or die by competing. Competition is a binary, win-lose survival mechanism.
    o Diversity. Slightly different characteristics of new generations of entities affect their ability to survive. Those with variations that fit best with the environmental conditions have a better chance of survival. Over time, entities will look and act very differently.
    o Innovation. Some variations in new generations cause an entity to compete in an entirely new way. If these variations increase the likelihood of survival, they will remain and be passed down to future generations.
    o Efficiency. Entities that can consume fewer resources or produce more offspring with the same resources are more efficient and increase their chances of survival when resources are scarce. Over time, more efficient entities will populate the world.

Chapter 6

Collaboration

How did entities outsmart competition? Duh. By doing the opposite of competing.

Competition pits entities against each other, resulting in winners and losers; therefore, the opposite approach would be joining with others to create a win-win situation. Over time, some cells joined together and worked toward a common goal, eliminating the need to compete.

I call this activity collaboration. Collaboration is the interaction between two or more units that results in an outcome neither unit could achieve by itself. We humans normally think of collaboration as having conscious intent. Nonhuman entities are not capable of intent. When we broaden the definition to include unintentional activities, we see that collaboration has been going on for a long time. A cell, in a sense, is a collaboration of inert materials that forms life.

Living entities act differently than the mere matter that preceded them. They transform matter into completely different matter. They break down the food they consume into energy and nutrients; they can even make copies of themselves. When energy is introduced into a cell, resources are transformed into completely different materials. It is the collaboration between inert matter and energy that enabled life to emerge. Single-celled entities are the bridge between matter and life. They're made of inert materials that collaborated to form a living entity.

Collaboration didn't happen overnight. It was a time-consuming process. Unlike competition, which was the immediate go-to survival mechanism, collaboration was a response to competition that took eons to develop. It took 750 million years for inert matter to collaborate into a prokaryote. It took another 1.8 billion years for the prokaryote's innards to collaborate into the highly organized eukaryote. Collaboration takes time.

Collaboration creates organization. Remember, the prokaryote was essentially a jumbled mess of matter inside a hard shell. A eukaryote contains all the same components as the prokaryote, but it's more organized. The components are no longer free to swim around the inside of the cell, like in a prokaryote. Instead, the parts of the eukaryote are fixed inside organelles and are free only to perform their specific function. In a sense, these organelles traded their freedom of movement for safety and nourishment.

Organization results in efficiency. The proteins and enzymes in a eukaryote are confined to specific locations and particular functions, so they use less energy to perform the same function than if they swam freely like they would if they were in a prokaryote. Over time, protected in their own tiny environments, the contents of organelles developed even more efficient ways of operating. We call this process specialization. Using specialization and strict compartmental separation, organelles evolved more intricate and efficient structures while using the same quantity or even fewer resources. The complex eukaryotes, with their specialized architecture, were so efficient that they dominated vast swaths of Earth's environment and pushed the prokaryotes into tight niches where only they could survive. Prokaryotes still exist. In fact, they dominate in pure numbers of organisms, even today, but they have hardly advanced past the one-celled stage. The disorganized internal structure keeps its optimal size at one cell, or, in some cases, a very small number of cells.

Between 600 million and one billion years ago, single-celled eukaryotes began to collaborate even more. They evolved into multicellular organisms. Scientists are not sure how they evolved. Some think individual cells of the same species joined together into clusters and, over time, added, deleted, or altered functions as the multicelled concoction grew bigger. Other scientists think that single-celled organisms transformed into multicelled entities over time. A glitch in copying could have created a conjoined entity that survived as a multicelled creature. Since individual cells already knew how to turn proteins on and off to make specific events happen at specific times, it's not hard to imagine that this capability could be revised to perform this activity across cells as well as inside them.

Perhaps there were other ways collaboration began. The point is eukaryotes developed a process that incorporated the entire DNA structure into each cell, yet the cells only performed specific functions to keep their part of the multicelled creature alive. This is the first case of collaboration between living entities. We are now over that bridge. Prokaryotes bridged matter and life. Multicelled eukaryotes involve life only.

Around the same time eukaryotes evolved, sexual reproduction emerged as a collaborative strategy. On the surface, sexual reproduction would appear to be an unlikely survival strategy. It takes more energy and time to produce offspring than asexual reproduction. Asexual reproduction involves an organism creating offspring identical to the parent. It uses the process of mitosis in which the cell's contents are meticulously copied, separated, and divided into two identical cells.

Sexual reproduction is a more complicated approach. A cell undergoes the process of meiosis, in which a full cell is divided into cells with slightly different DNA. In sexual reproduction, each parent contributes half the genetic code, which already means the offspring will have different DNA than either parent. The genetic code, or genome, is a cell's entire DNA strand. It is stored in a body's chromosomes. These chromosomes perform an unusual activity once initially joined during sexual intercourse—they mix themselves up before settling into a chromosome slot. It's a little like kids playing musical chairs, but when the music stops, there's a chair for everyone, but just not the chair the child started with. This shake-up forces the joined cells to differ even more from their parents, even though all offspring share the exact same DNA. The offspring exhibit different characteristics depending on how the chromosomes are arranged. The cells then divide again and create four cells. Two of these cells become female egg cells, and the other two become male sperm cells. When a male and female engage in sexual activity, they are assured of producing offspring with an even wider variety of characteristics. Okay, I get it. That was probably the least romantic discussion of sex ever. Sorry, not sorry.

Compared to asexual reproduction, sexual reproduction is much more complicated and energy expensive. It evolved because it improved an entity's chance of survival. If an organism exists in a competitive environment, sexual reproduction guarantees the production of offspring with different characteristics. Even if only a few survive, they and their method of reproduction will survive to procreate another day. On the other hand, if the asexual organism cannot withstand a harsh environment, its identical offspring will likely fare no better. The organism may die, leaving one less organism practicing asexual reproduction in the environment.

Sexual reproduction is an example of collaboration. It also speeds up diversification. Instead of waiting for variations to appear as mutations, the cell creates variations as part of the procreative process. As each new generation was born into the competitive environment, variation and change accelerated dramatically.

Around 600 million years ago, a particular model of multicelled entity emerged. We can conclude that it was more efficient than all the other models that arose because all of today's eukaryotic creatures share this model. The structures of fish and bees and humans are remarkably similar—far more similar than different. They all possess brains and hearts and appendages and circulatory systems. Although they appear quite different on the outside, they operate similarly on the inside because they all emerged from a common ancestor embodying this basic structure.

From that basic structure, a multitude of complex entities have emerged. Cells did not stop collaborating because they existed in multicellular units. They continued to produce more efficient functions and perform more specialized roles. Complex entities produced groups of cells called tissues. Cells in tissues then collaborated to form larger units called organs. Each new collaboration resulted in more specialized functions: hearts to pump blood, kidneys to process waste, stomachs to convert raw resources into building materials and energy. All these organs are made up of cells that share identical DNA but operate very differently.

With every functional change, the structure of the creatures changed to help them better fit into their environment. They developed legs for moving on land, fins and gills for living in water, tails for balance, and fur for warmth.

There is one additional level of collaboration more complex than bodies: colonies. Ants and bees have evolved to live in colonies. A colony is a relatively rare formation in nature, one in which the individual entities collaborate to ensure the colony survives. Feeding baby bees or ants different amounts of food after hatching produces entities that perform different functions: foragers, guards, caregivers, or queens. In a sense, the colony acts like a living entity, and the individuals act more like cells within a body. Those individual bees do what collaborative cells do—they give up some of their freedom to specialize in one function. In turn, they receive protection and nourishment from all the other ants or bees performing their functions.

When cells collaborate, it makes it impossible for them to compete. When cells join to form a complex creature, they work together for the benefit of each other and the creature itself. Competing against one another would provide no benefit, only harm. The reprieve is only temporary though. Competition does not disappear; it just rises to the level where the complex creature can exist as an independent unit. The heart of a tiger beats and its stomach processes food, but the tiger now must compete with other entities that consume the same resources it does. If the tiger does not eat, it does not survive, and the whole collaborative structure—heart, stomach, and every single cell that makes up that tiger—dies.

Interdependence

Collaborative cells are interdependent. The cells within tissues and organs in a body are alive; they are composed of living cells, but they can't function without the rest of the cells in the body. The cells of a tiger are not just linked; they are utterly dependent on each other. Cut out the heart, a living organ made only of living cells, and the whole animal dies.

Mutual Benefit

Collaboration can only exist if mutual benefit exists. Every cell in a body makes a trade: it performs its function in exchange for food and safety. It's a win-win. Mutual benefit is symbiotic. Not only does each cell function and survive, but they also work together to create a body, which would not exist without the collaboration of the cells.

Specialization

Over time, collaborative cells always specialize. Even though a cell within a body is protected from competition, variations still occur at the cellular level. Like all variations, the more efficient ones help the body survive, and the less efficient ones reduce the chances of survival. Consider a heart. It was a single tube in small, multicellular organisms 600 million years ago. When the first fish evolved 420 million years ago, the heart had become a two-chambered pump. In modern humans, the heart is a sophisticated four-chambered system. Over time, tissues and organs evolved into more efficient members of the body. Once a complex form evolves, it becomes the basis for even further changes. Life produces efficiency through complexity rather than through simplicity.

With these changes, the actual structure of bodies changed too. Creatures developed different bodily structures based on their different environments. Fish and bees and spiders and tigers all look different, despite having similar basic structures, because each is specialized to fit into its environment.

Survival is a delicate dance between competition and collaboration. At every level of life, there is a symphony of these two. The inner workings of a cell, the tissues and organs of complex plants and animals, the members of a hive—they're all collaborative units spurred on by the pressures of outside competition.

Competition and collaboration work together to make a body function. Which is more successful? If we consider all life forms on Earth, we find that more cells collaborate than compete. While it's true that there are more single-celled organisms than multicelled ones, multicellular creatures are so much larger and contain so many cells that the collaborating cells far outnumber the cells in single-celled organisms.

Collaboration has resulted in some very complex entities. Humans contain 35 trillion cells. Which begs the question: How the heck do all of your 35 trillion cells work together to keep you alive?

Keys to Unlocking the Ideasphere:
- Collaboration is a survival mechanism that was a response to the pressures of competition.
- Collaboration took much longer to develop than competition.
- Collaboration is the interaction of two or more units that results in an outcome neither unit could achieve by itself.
- Collaboration is another word for organization. Collaborative units are organized units.
- All life forms utilize collaboration. Cell parts collaborate to make a cell alive. Cells collaborate to make a multicelled unit. Even some multicelled units collaborate to create colonies.
- Sexual reproduction is a collaborative action that ensures offspring will vary from their parents.
- Collaboration produces outcomes different than those of competition:
    - Mutual Benefit: All cells trade their independence for the security and nourishment of a larger collaborative body. In exchange, they perform their limited function 24/7 for the benefit of the other cells and the body as a whole.

- Interdependence: All cells must do their job for the body to survive. The cell can't survive without all the other cells doing their job. If the body dies, all the cells die too.
- Specialization: Life constantly evolves and changes, including individual cells inside a complex body. Cells that make changes that enhance the cells' and body's survival will be carried forward to a new generation. Cells that make changes that are detrimental to the body's survival may damage or kill the body and thus not be carried forward to a new generation. Over time, complex entities with specialized functions make life forms look and act very differently.

Chapter 7

Coordination

For collaboration to work in a complex body, all the cells need to do their jobs in the right way and at the right time. The cells need to be coordinated. Coordination enables all the different parts of a body to work together to achieve a goal. Coordination is a type of collaboration. However, because coordination behaves very differently than typical collaboration, it's better to think of it as a separate survival mechanism.

We can think of competition and collaboration as a set of actions that a creature takes to survive. Coordination, on the other hand, is the mechanism that keeps all the parts of the creature working together. No living organism can exist without coordination. It has been part of life ever since the first life forms evolved.

Even prokaryotes contained a coordination mechanism, though it was rudimentary. Cells developed receptors, stringy proteins with one end perched outside the cell membrane and the other inside the cell membrane. When the receptor encountered a chemical signal in the environment, the receptor emitted its own chemical signals that caused the DNA inside the cell to turn on or turn off a specific protein. If the cell responded in a way that improved its ability to survive, the cell response was copied into the next generation by copying the successful DNA configuration. The cells that did not perform this function well lost the survival race. The DNA, in a sense, served as the coordinator.

Over time, some cells created a web of receptors that covered the outer surface of the cell. They detected external stimuli on a continuous basis and sent messages to the interior cell for a response. With millions and millions of years to work with, prokaryotes developed an efficient, fine-tuned ability to sense and respond to their environment.

This is the genius of a cell. Each cell component plays a tiny role. A receptor interacts with the environment, passing the information to a protein, which passes it to another protein, which passes it to another, and so on, until the DNA responds, and the cell survives or not. Tiny parts, each carrying tiny loads, make tiny changes. Over and over and over. Eventually, these ever-changing cells evolved into huge, complex creatures. At every step, coordination was key to them working as a unit. Given enough time, the parts could transform into all kinds of creatures, as long as those parts could communicate with each other.

Eukaryotes converted the rudimentary receptors of the prokaryotes into more structured forms. They evolved ways to use a wider variety of chemicals to improve connections between signaling proteins. As eukaryotes evolved into multicellular organisms, the messaging system became even more sophisticated with the incorporation of electrical signals. Over time, multicellular creatures transformed receptors and signaling proteins into cells that transmitted information. We call these transmitter cells neurons. That system of neurons became the nervous system, or the neural system.

Receptors of the prokaryotes evolved into sense organs in multicellular entities, such as eyes and ears and noses. Near these organs, a large cluster of neurons developed to process the continuous flow of information coming from these sense organs. That is the brain.

The brain is a large cluster of neurons, which, remember, are all cells with the same DNA as the rest of the body. In every multicelled creature, the neural system takes information from the outside world—like images you see, sounds you hear, aromas you smell, and objects you touch—and converts them into electrical signals that are then passed from one neuron cell to another until they arrive at the brain. The brain then processes all these signals and translates them into a response. Signals are then sent back through the neural system to cells throughout the body to implement the response.

Though every brain is different, they all function in a similar way. And they share the same goal—to enhance the body's chance of survival.

Each neural system evolved to meet the needs of the creature it supported. A bee's brain has a volume of two cubic millimeters and contains one million neurons. Bees use their brains to process environmental conditions from their sense organs, mainly optical images and odors. They are also able to communicate the locations of food resources to others in the hive.

Fish have about ten million neurons in their brains. Their brain size varies according to their body size. Even though they live in water and ingest oxygen via water entering through gills, something other animals cannot do, their brains are quite similar to other eukaryotic brains.

Humans have about 100 billion neurons. When we compare brain size to body size, humans have the largest brain mass-to-body mass ratio of all animals. The large human brain is very significant, as we shall soon see.

Coordination efforts have even evolved outside of bodies. A bee colony is an example of higher-level coordination. The colony is the "complex body" that must be nurtured for survival. The queen acts as the coordinating system and ensures that enough bees exist in every role so that the hive survives. The bees are like cells inside a body, each performing a specific function to ensure the hive survives. If the hive survives, they survive. A colony is a collaborative structure orchestrated by the queen coordinator.

Collaboration cannot exist without coordination. The actions of the neural system ensure that cells work together properly so that both the cells and the entity survive. If something happens to the body—an injury or an accident, for example—the neural system goes into action to make sure the body and its cells survive.

Characteristics

The characteristics of the neural system are particularly important, especially when we talk about humans. These traits are essential for the cells to get along together in the body. And they provide valuable clues about how humans can get along in societies.

Protection

Though the coordinating system is composed of the same cells as the other cells in the entity, it is physically separate from them. Bones and tissue layers surround the brain and nervous system, protecting them from injury that other cells may cause. The neural system evolved its protective covering to make sure that any negative outcomes resulting from its actions do not impair its ability to function. For instance, the neural system may direct white blood cells to kill off cells infected with a virus. The protective tissues prevent any detritus from getting to the neural system and affecting its ability to function properly.

Nourishment

The brain is nourished as all other cells are; it gets no preferential treatment. Despite its critical role, nourishment is meted out in a body according to the needs of every cell. However, the neural system does receive its nourishment first. It doesn't take more than it needs, but it gets nourished first to ensure it has enough energy to maintain control over all the body's cells.

Reporting

In a complex organism, every single cell in the body continually transmits data about its status to other cells. This data is in the form of proteins or enzymes or amino acids. Some of the data enters the neural system, where the messages are sent to the brain. The brain processes this stream of data and sends back its own messages, specifying a response. Coordination is impossible without the constant flow of information sent by the individual cells reporting on their status.

Neural systems vary in different life forms so that the creatures can exist in different environments. Regardless of how brains evolved and how different they are, they all generally work the same way. The neural system sets a goal, establishes rules, and enforces those rules. Let's look at these jobs more closely.

Goals

For coordination to be successful, the complex organism must have a goal or a purpose. This looks an awful lot like intentional behavior, but I assure you it is not. Humans can set goals, but nonhumans cannot—they inherit their goals.

Nonhumans do not make decisions; they can only follow the instructions dictated by their DNA. When a creature follows its instructions, it either survives or dies. If it survives, it goes on. If it does not survive, it is out. Permanently. It is gone. Its DNA is gone. It is forever lost to the earth. So, at any one point in time, the only creatures that exist are survivors. Given that entities cannot make decisions and can only follow instructions in their DNA, we can conclude that by following their DNA instructions, entities survive. In other words, we can say that DNA instructions lead to survival. Since only survivors ever exist, we must conclude that survival is the goal. There is literally no other goal around. All the creatures with other goals, if they even had them, died. In the end, nothing else matters except that an entity survives. The creature's coordinating function didn't set the goal; it inherited the goal from billions of generations of survivors.

The neural system is unique among the body's organs because it does not directly participate in the survival functions of the entity. It doesn't pump blood or convert food into energy. All it does is coordinate the work of the other cells. Given how relatively large and energy expensive brains are, it seems counterintuitive that they would form at all. Yet form they did. Why? Why do most changes in life occur? Because having a central coordinating mechanism was a more efficient use of energy than having each cell in a body try to coordinate their actions on their own.

Rules

It is not enough for a body to have goals. It must also have a set of rules that all cells can follow. As with the goal, cells inherit their rules from their DNA. In every cell, responses are encoded inside DNA. When a signal is passed along the neural path, the last protein in line causes the DNA to respond. The DNA instructs RNA to make a protein, or stop making a protein, or respond in some other way. RNA follows the DNA's specific instruction, which is the response to the incoming information. This is how the incoming signal connects to the response; this is how a body follows the rules.

The cell works without any conditions. Cells only do what they are instructed to do. When A happens, B is the programmed response. The more often a cell produces the same beneficial response to a stimulus, the more likely the cell is to survive. A cell that produces a beneficial response but is unable to repeat it when the stimulus occurs again is less likely to survive than one with more consistent repetition ability.

Enforcement

Rules are worthless unless they're enforced. Enforcement in entities works like all the other coordinating functions—it is inherited. When a cell survives because it follows the rules in its DNA, the rule is enforced. If a cell dies or is damaged because it followed the rules in its DNA, the rule is also enforced, just in the opposite way.

Billions of signals move around in a complex body at any given moment. Every cell regularly sends information to the brain regarding its survival status. With so many signals, the odds are quite good that unpredictable responses will occur. Built into all coordination systems is the capability to detect and correct problems. Proteins and enzymes exist within all cells to detect a problem. If the problem is small, say a small puncture wound, the neural system activates nearby enzymes to close the puncture. Other proteins are instructed to work with the DNA of the injured cell to regenerate new parts to replace the damaged ones. In this case, the neural system takes action to repair the cells. In a sense, it enforces the rule that cells function properly.

If a cell endures significant injury and cannot be repaired, the neural system activates proteins and enzymes within the cell to initiate the process to kill itself with as little damage to the rest of the body as possible. The cell shrinks, the nucleus breaks up, the DNA fractures into small pieces, and the cell surface changes. The neural system also activates nearby phagocytes, cells that are present in tissues but are usually inactive, to step in and absorb these pieces and recycle them for use by other cells. In this case, the neural system enforces the rules in a different way. Since the cell cannot be repaired, it is not allowed to play on Team Body. It is killed, and its parts are recycled.

If a cell receives an acute injury, such as from an accident, it may die instantly. When this happens, it spills its contents all over its cellular neighborhood. In this case, the neural system responds by sending white blood cells from other locations to clean up the mess. Swelling, pain, and tissue redness often result. In this case, the neural system takes enforcement action to protect as many cells as possible.

No matter the situation, the neural system works to keep as many cells as possible alive and functioning properly.

Coordination is stunningly complex. In a chess game, with 64 spaces and 32 game pieces, about 10^{40} legal moves are possible. That's one with 40 zeros after it. A human body contains 35 trillion cells, of which 100 billion are neurons. Just think of all the possible interactions that occur. And all, or at least most, must work properly for a human to survive.

Coordination takes a lot of energy. If an entity with an expensive neural system can use its coordinating capabilities to obtain enough resources to allow it to "pay for" its brain use and still create offspring, that entity has an advantage that is then handed down to the next generation. At some point, a trade-off occurs. If a brain grows so big that the body cannot obtain enough resources for other functions, its chances of survival may decrease. On the other hand, if the brain is so small it cannot support complex functions, the entity may never grow big or complex enough to protect itself from predators. Brain development is a trade-off between size and complexity. It all depends on the environment. Each creature can only spend as much energy on coordination as the competitive and collaborative environment allows.

Coordination re-establishes the accountability that can be lost in collaboration. Cells in a body do not need to compete for their survival, but they are required to perform their functions to remain as part of the body. The neural system ensures that every cell does its part.

Every life form has a coordinating system. Ironically, the earth itself does not have a neural system, a force that coordinates all living things in its sphere. Every living thing coexists on the planet without any overall coordination. Entities compete and collaborate without coordination because that's all they can do.

This makes sense.

Life evolved by branching out. Ever since life emerged, creatures have grown increasingly complex and diverse. Each change has accumulated to make them less alike. To coordinate, life forms need to communicate. And to do that, they require similar mechanisms for communication. It would have been far too energy expensive for creatures to develop communication capabilities, especially when they were evolving on separate paths. Divergence, difference, diversity—that is how creatures journeyed through time. The only time all of us were capable of being united under one banner of mutual understanding and communication was when our ancestors were prokaryotes.

Keys to Understanding the Ideasphere:
- Coordination is the mechanism that keeps all the parts of a lifeform working together.
- No living organism can exist without coordination.
- Coordination requires communication.
- The coordinating function in multicelled creatures is the neural system, which is made up of the brain and the nervous system that transmits signals between the body and the brain.
- All coordination systems have these characteristics in common:
    o The neural system is protected from outside influence by the other cells.
    o The coordination system assures that all cells are nourished as they need.
    o All cells continuously report their status to the neural system.
- All coordination systems work the same way:
    o The neural system "sets the goal" of survival, which is embedded in the DNA of all nonhuman creatures.

- o The neural system "establishes the rules" by which all cells must operate. This is also embedded in the DNA.
  - o The neural system "enforces the rules" by either helping a cell act the way it's supposed to or by killing a cell that is unable to act as it is supposed to.
- Coordination requires a lot of energy.
- Coordination re-establishes accountability between cells and the body.
- Earth does not have a coordination system.

Chapter 8

Information

We can think of survival as successful information processing. Information is at the core of all life. All living entities survive because they process information, and every creature processes information in its cells, or more precisely, in the DNA of its cells. This is why DNA is so important.

All cells process information the same way. First, they store information in a stable location. Second, they process data and generate a response. Third, they store the response in the stable location.

Let's start with a few definitions. What is information? Information is useful data. Which begs the question: What is data? Data is something that exists and has a particular arrangement or sequence. That's a little confusing, so let's use an example. Think of a rock. A rock is data. Every characteristic of that rock is also data. It is a thing with a particular arrangement of characteristics. The sum of all those characteristics defines our rock. Data, as defined, is scattered everywhere in the universe, not just in rocks. All the things in the universe that are not life are data. Every hydrogen atom, every molecule, every star, every planet, every bit of energy sitting around in the universe—all is data. All nonliving things contain characteristics that we define as data. These characteristics, in turn, define the essence of the thing.

For data to become information, it must become useful. Before life formed, nothing existed that could "use" the characteristics of our rock. Water does not care what a rock is made of. It just flows over the rock every day until the rock erodes into tiny grains of sand. The water doesn't behave any differently with the sand than it did with the rock. It just flows onto the sand every day, carrying it in and out on the tide. The nature of rock and sand is useless to water. The nature of water is useless to rock and sand. These are just data-filled objects running into each other. Data is useless to nonliving objects.

The evolution of life changed this framework. Life forms can identify conditions in the environment and respond to them. When an entity can respond to data embedded in an object, then that data becomes useful to the entity. The data becomes information.

For information to be useful, it must be able to be stored, and the storage method must be reliable and protected. Let's say you own an old-fashioned address book. The addresses and phone numbers inside the book are useful to you. They represent the means by which you contact your friends. Therefore, these numbers qualify as information. If you use super flimsy paper that tears when you open the book or a pen with ink that smears all the numbers, the address book isn't protected or reliable, so its usefulness is severely limited.

DNA is the address book of the cell. The DNA holds all the instructions necessary to produce any materials the cell needs to survive. DNA is a stable molecule and is protected inside the nucleus. It cannot break apart unless it is hit with a burst of energy. Even if it does break apart, it immediately finds its missing pieces in the cell and reforms its original shape. DNA is the equivalent of a good, sturdy address book that won't lose its pages or smear its entries.

DNA strands are grouped into genes. Genes are aligned in a particular pattern that, when activated, can start, process, and then stop a particular action, the creation of a specific protein, for example. Genes function like small computer programs that produce a single instruction. We can think of the entire DNA strand as a collection of genes that together produce all the instructions the cell needs to survive. Scientists call this the genome. All the instructions the cell needs to survive are in the DNA inside the genes inside the genome. The genome is the information storage area with each DNA molecule holding a piece of the actual information the cell needs to live.

When we open our address book and look up a number, we do the same thing a cell does when an enzyme hits the genome noting a change in the environment—it processes information. Every living entity processes information. There are no exceptions. From the tiniest one-celled organism to the biggest blue whale, they all do it the same way, via the DNA in their cells. Information processing only appears different because life comes in so many different forms. Over the eons, each living entity adapted its information processing system to fit its particular set of environmental conditions, but the process is fundamentally the same. Here's how it works:

First, an entity receives input from the environment using its receptors. Second, the receptors convert the data from the environment into a signal the neural system can recognize. Third, the neural system transmits the signal to the brain. Fourth, the neurons in the brain determine a response. Fifth, the neurons send the response back through the neural system. Lastly, the entity's cells respond.

Let's go back to our address book for a moment. The address book sits in a drawer, protected and stable until it is needed. That's equivalent to our genome sitting inside the nucleus. When you decide to call a friend, you go to the drawer, pull out the address book, and leaf through the pages until you find your friend's name. That's analogous to an enzyme strolling down the genome until it finds the particular gene holding the DNA molecule required for a response. You pick up the phone, dial your friend's number, and proceed to talk. This is equivalent to the enzyme reacting with the gene and causing a reaction that results in RNA making (or not making) a particular protein. When you're done with the call, you close the address book and return it to the drawer. This is equivalent to the genome reverting to its original form.

Let's go one step further. When you put the address book away, you know that you can still reach your friend by using their entry in the address book. That is similar to how the cell operates. If the response enables the cell to survive, we can conclude that this information processing event was beneficial to survival. Every time that response is made, the cell continues to survive. This is a positive feedback loop. The cell's response confirmed that the DNA response should be maintained. We can think of the response itself as being stored in the DNA, because whenever a similar stimulus occurs, the DNA responds in this same way to benefit the cell.

Now, let's look at the reverse scenario. Suppose you couldn't reach your friend by dialing that number. You cannot communicate with your friend. This is analogous to a harmful response in our cell. The flow of information resulted in a harmful, or at best, a non-beneficial response. Now the cell's chances of survival decrease. This is a negative feedback loop. Even if the cell survives this negative result, if the DNA continues to respond to the same stimulus with the same negative outcome, the cell will eventually die.

Over time, the cells with positive feedback loops survive, and the ones with negative feedback loops disappear. We can conclude that creatures who survive have DNA information storage systems that encourage survival. In essence, those positive responses to external conditions enable creatures to fit within their environment.

Stimuli constantly hit a cell's receptors. Numerous messages stream into the cell. The genome continuously responds to these messages, which leads to multiple simultaneous changes in the cell. With so much activity going on at once, the cell is in a constant state of flux. So, it's not just one change that affects a cell's survival, but a constant stream of changes. It stands to reason that, over time, the cell with DNA that can consistently create more positive responses from a myriad of stimuli is more likely to survive.

When humans store the results of their experiences and act on them in the future, we call that learning. Every single cell on this earth works the same way, so we can say that every cell learns. And every creature learns. Nonhuman learning is not a conscious act; it is derived from the results of the DNA's prior successful actions.

Of all the responses that DNA attempts, only those with positive outcomes allow the cell to survive. Negative outcomes result in death. Survival in cells is therefore the result of positive experiences repeatedly produced by DNA. Since, over time, the cells with negative experiences died out, the cells that exist today contain DNA with primarily positive experiences.

DNA is like a library. The genome of a cell is the configuration of an entity's most current state of information as well as its accumulated experience. The library isn't perfect, as we well know. If there is a sudden environmental change, the cells may lack the necessary experience to deal with the new conditions. If it can't use its current responses to keep it alive, it will die, just like the dinosaurs died when the Chicxulub asteroid hit.

In animals, "instinct" refers to experiences that have been incorporated into the DNA of their cells. Learning is the incorporation of experience that can be repeated. Humans think of learning as a conscious human act, but with nonhumans, we must think more broadly. Nonhumans learn; they just don't know they do it. When an animal is born, it comes loaded with DNA that previous generations honed into a set of responses that heretofore ensured survivability. There is literally no other place to store information than in the DNA of a cell. Over the eons that organisms existed, they incorporated every beneficial living behavior, i.e., instinct, into the only place they could keep and reuse it: in the DNA of their cells. When a bird builds a nest or a tiger chases an okapi or a mother polar bear protects her cubs, they are following successful instructions from billions of years of evolution that have proven to increase their chances of survival.

Learning is the process of accumulating experience as information. Memory is the expression of previously learned information. Every living thing can "learn," that is, accumulate experience and store it as information to be called on for later use. Memory is the activation of the stored information for present use. Every living entity possesses memory. Memory is the activation of particular neurons in a particular order that are stored in the brain. The more well-traveled the neuron path from stimulus to storage, the stronger the memory. When stimuli come in, signals are sent to neurons in the brain to determine if any past experiences related to the stimuli should be activated. If so, a particular set of neurons is activated, and the memory is recalled. Just as every creature can learn, every creature possesses a memory.

All changes in living beings result from DNA's ability to process information. No matter how complex a living entity becomes, it can only store and process information within the DNA of the cell. In a complex body, cascades of messages are sent to DNA every second. It stands to reason that, occasionally, some messages might get garbled. Whenever a different DNA strand is produced, a different type of entity is produced. If the change enables the "garbled" cell to operate more efficiently, then the cell might survive and pass that change on to its offspring. Over billions of years, a single prokaryote's DNA can be transformed to become the DNA of a eukaryote, and with more time, yeast, and with even more time, a bee or a tiger or a human.

Evolution of life moves toward efficiency. Ironically, life does not produce optimally efficient life forms. Change occurs step by step. Human hearts evolved from simple pumping mechanisms adapted by early life forms. A human heart was not designed by a "Life Engineering Team." If it had been, it would be a clean, elegant, highly efficient model that pumps blood economically, not the convoluted assortment of crosswise tubes and chambers that exist today. Evolution is not engineered. Every change results from an earlier version that was previously suitable in its environment. Each minor modification must adapt to fit. Adaption doesn't guarantee the model will be the most efficient, only that it will be more efficient than the previous version.

The feedback process, which is the foundation of information processing, is how the neural system re-establishes accountability in collaborative bodies. An entity can only follow the instructions in its DNA. Whatever happens, happens. Regardless of the outcome, positive or negative, the entity bears the burden of the result. By processing information, an entity either survives or dies. That is the very definition of accountability.

Information processing occurs within the cells. The risk of death or the benefit of survival plays out at the cellular level. The body containing the cells just goes along for the ride. If enough cells process information well, the body survives. Competition and collaboration are different contexts in which the cell operates. Cells compete or cells collaborate, but underlying both is information processing. Competition and collaboration are survival mechanisms. It's the information processing in DNA that is the underlying foundation of all life.

In a complex body, like a tiger or a human, it is the cells of the neural system that use information. Complex bodies need large amounts of energy to survive. If every one of the 35 trillion cells in a human body must work together to make the body work, every one of those 35 trillion cells must be fed and nourished. Bodies take in resources, convert them into energy and nutrients, and distribute them to the rest of the body via the bloodstream. Every cell receives the nourishment it needs so it can do its job—that is, process incoming information and produce the necessary proteins to keep its portion of the body working. Neurons, especially the neurons in the brain, use a vast amount of energy to maintain the feedback loop between all the body's cells. Constant signaling depletes neurons, so for them to keep working, they must continuously recharge their energy stores. In humans, brains account for only 3% of the body's mass but consume 20% of the energy a body takes in. That's far more energy than any other organ uses.

I could make a joke that some folks don't use the whole 20%. But I won't.

Keys to Understanding the Ideasphere:
- Data is a description of all the characteristics of a thing.
- Information is data that is useful to a life form.
- All living entities survive by processing information.
- To be useful, information must be storable, reliable, and generate a repeatable response.
- All information in living bodies is stored in the cell's DNA.

- Information processing works the same way in all creatures:
    - Information is stored in the DNA of all cells
    - When an external stimulus is received, a message is sent to the DNA
    - The DNA determines a response
    - The response is sent through the neural system to the cells
    - The cells respond
    - The cells live or die as a result
- Information processing is a feedback loop. A positive feedback loop enables a cell to survive, and a negative feedback loop causes injury or death. Over time, only creatures with positive feedback loops exist. The feedback loop creates accountability in every cell in a body.
- Storing accumulated experience is called learning. All creatures learn. Instinct in nonhumans is an unintentional learned behavior that has accumulated in the cell's DNA, the only place in the natural world where information can be stored.
- Memory is accessing learned information for present use.
- All change results from information processing. When a variation is produced, a different creature emerges. Different DNA, different creature. Over time, many diverse creatures have formed.
- Change generally produces more efficient life forms—not the most efficient life forms possible, but more efficient than the previous version.

Chapter 9

The World Before Humans

It is now time to stop and review all the matters we have discussed so far. Let's take a look at the world before humans emerged.

Two hundred thousand years ago, which is about the time Homo sapiens emerged, the earth was already a 4.5-billion-year-old planet that had undergone numerous violent changes. It was covered with about 70% water and 30% land. It had a temperate climate that varied between 0 and 100 degrees Celsius. Life forms inhabited both land and ocean.

Trillions and quadrillions of single-celled organisms could be found everywhere on Earth—in water, in dirt, and even inside the bodies of complex creatures, like bees and tigers and fish. These one-celled organisms were composed of distinctive bits of matter that all worked together to make the cell a living entity. Each cell had a feedback loop that enabled it to receive, transmit, and respond to stimuli in its surroundings. Single-celled organisms competed with other organisms for resources in order to survive.

Millions and billions of complex creatures existed on Earth alongside the single-celled organisms. These were entities like plants and bees and tigers. Their cells were grouped into organs and tissues and neural systems that all worked together to keep the body working and surviving as a unit. The creature formed from those cells competed for resources at its level. The cells collaborated to keep the body alive and did not compete with one another. The cells in the brain and nervous system kept all the cells working together. We can see that in every complex organism, competition, collaboration, and coordination all work together.

Bees and ants evolved to form colonies. In some ways, colonies could be considered an entity of their own, but it was a loose structure at best. Colonies did not have cells; only the individual bees did. However, the individual bees acted like "cells" when performing in service of the colony. The queen bee was the coordinator. She determined how many and what type of workers would live in the colony by feeding bees different amounts of nectar and pollen. She was the colony's "neural system." The bees acted like collaborative cells in a body. Each had a job to do that enabled the colony to survive and thrive. As a group, the individual bees competed with other entities for food. They competed with other bee colonies or with birds, but these bees were still individuals with their own cells and DNA. So, at this level too, we see that the individuals that formed a colony competed, collaborated, and coordinated to survive.

Above the colony level, there was no collaboration or coordination. Some species coexisted in a mutually beneficial way, but they weren't coordinated. There was no "natural" United Nations where all creatures came together to hash out the world's problems. Each species evolved its own path through the chain of life, diverging from one another as time passed. So all they were left with at this highest level was competition.

Two hundred thousand years ago, Earth had a finely tuned set of competitors, each of whom fit their environment and could be predators in some cases and prey in others. Every member of the ecosystem followed their DNA instructions to secure resources and produce offspring so that they, and their DNA, would survive. It was the ultimate feedback loop. An entity either survived in the ecosystem network or it did not. If a catastrophic environmental change occurred, survival was not guaranteed.

Earth appeared to be a serenely balanced system. Balanced, yes, but serene, it was not. Every member was constantly under pressure to balance resource availability, competitor capability, and predator presence. If a creature managed to eat enough resources, avoid being eaten, and convert its excess energy into offspring, its DNA would survive. The ecosystem was not a well-oiled machine being operated by some invisible hand. The ecosystem was a chaotic free-for-all with each member striving to survive with the instructions it received from its ancestors. Second to second, minute to minute, hour to hour, day to day, year to year, century to century, millennium to millennium, eon to eon, the ecosystem was ever-changing, one tiny step at a time.

At the base of all this life was DNA, the information holder. A cell took in data and sent it to the DNA, where DNA instructed genes to turn on or off. The DNA then retained the results as information.

We can think of life at this time as nothing more than a vehicle for storing, changing, and re-storing information. Here on Earth, where life originated this way, it was the information, that is, the DNA, that was important, not the complex bodies that carried it. This comports with the history of life as we know it. DNA has held dominance for billions of years and continues to dominate by transforming itself into a myriad of different configurations that we call plants and animals. They all look and act differently, but they are, when it comes right down to it, unique bundles of one thing: DNA.

To expand on this concept, we can view all life that existed at that time as the present state of information on Earth. If a piece of DNA from every living thing on the planet could be gathered in one place, it would represent the total of all information that existed at that time. Now, that is not to say that this was the totality of all information that ever existed on Earth. Not at all. In fact, more creatures have lived and died during the existence of Earth than are alive today. Therefore, we can also say that more information has lived and died than all the information that existed at that moment 200,000 years ago. Fossils reveal only a glimpse of the information that has been lost during Earth's 4.5-billion-year lifespan. All we can say is that all living entities at that time represented the current state of information on Earth.

This is how Earth existed up until 200,000 years ago. All the information in the world existed in the sum total of all the living things on Earth. Then humans came along. It was humans who completely upended this framework. Humans . . . and their ideas.

PART 3

ECOSYSTEM 2

The Ideasphere: Humans and Ideas

Chapter 10

Humans

Between 80 and 55 million years ago, primates split off from the mammalian branch of the family, which included small animals that ate bugs and lived in trees. What I really mean is that the set of DNA modifications in the offspring of these animals was distinct enough to produce an entire line of creatures with those same distinct characteristics. The primate group continued to splinter, with new generations exhibiting various structures and characteristics. Some splinter groups evolved opposable thumbs and big toes, flexible shoulder joints, stereoscopic vision, and upright stature. About 200,000 years ago, the group we call Homo sapiens emerged from this branch. They had all these above-mentioned qualities, with one especially distinguishing characteristic: they had big brains. Really big brains. With these large brains, Homo sapiens began to do more than just process stimuli. About 50,000 years ago, they began to do something no other animal could do. They began to think.

No one knows exactly how it happened, but it's possible to surmise a sequence based on how other life forms evolved. We can be reasonably confident that it started simply, like all new elements of life. Initially, humans developed the ability to notice and identify the things around them and link them to their survival. For instance, they might observe that their surroundings appear different during daytime versus nighttime. They might observe that large animals are more dangerous than small ones. Like other entities, they accumulated these observations as experience.

These observations didn't affect a human's DNA as they produced new generations. This is where humans evolved differently than other creatures. This is where they used those big brains. Using their large brains, humans developed a way to communicate outside their cells. We know cells must communicate with each other for a body to work as a unit. For humans to live together and work as a social unit, they need to be able to communicate like cells in a body. How did humans perform this amazing feat? They used their ability to think and created language.

Language is vitally important. Language enabled humans to collaborate and live together in bands or tribes.

Let's say an individual figured out that when the bright, shiny yellow object appeared in the sky, the air was light and warm, and when the bright, shiny yellow object did not appear in the sky, it was dark and cold. That information can be useful, but if it cannot be shared with others in the tribe, it is merely data. Before long, tribal members began to associate a specific gesture or sound with objects in their surroundings. For instance, they decided to call that yellow object "sun" and the blue area above their heads "sky." It didn't really matter what they called these objects, as long as all members agreed on the same sound for the same object. So, language can be defined as a human gesture or sound that describes a commonly experienced thing. Language shortcuts the need to wait for cells to incorporate learning into their DNA.

To form language, humans must think. They must translate a physical object or event they observe into a gesture or word. On one end of the translation is a physical object, and on the other end is a sound. It's a sound a human creates in their mind and then says out loud. The sound is not important in and of itself, but it becomes important when it's linked to the physical object it describes.

Human thinking is the process of creating ideas. When a human decided to give the bright yellow object up above the label "sun," that human created an idea. Previously, there was no link between the object and the sound. It only existed because a human conjured it up from inside their brain. When all the members of the tribe agreed on the label, they shared this idea. The sound "sun" means nothing in and of itself, but once everyone agreed to the sound-to-object link, the term "sun" became meaningful. Language is the set of all the gestures or sounds that represent shared ideas.

With time, humans became more adept at processing ideas into language. They began to expand beyond just naming physical phenomena. If you can name a sun, why can't you also name how it feels when the sun shines on you? You can say it is "hot" when the sun shines on you or "cold" when the sun does not shine on you. A human can't see "hot" or "cold." Those are abstract ideas based on the experience of being hot or cold. But if all humans agree on a sound to represent hot and cold, they can communicate about an abstract concept that doesn't even exist in the physical world. Those abstract ideas can now be shared and become the basis for even more ideas. This is the power of language and of human thought.

Once humans created words for things, tangible or intangible, they could add additional words to create even more complex ideas. They might put together that when the sun is in a certain part of the sky, it's hot, and when the sun is in a different part of the sky, it's cold. Then they might be able to act on that thought, maybe wearing an animal hide when the sun is at the cold angle. Later, they could come up with even more complex ideas, like "Why is there a sun anyway?" Once thinking started, it didn't stop.

Around 5,000 years ago, humans made another significant change. They began to record their ideas in an external form. They learned to write. Once they had connected an idea to a sound, it was not a huge leap to connect an idea to a drawn symbol. This development also likely started simply.

First came the idea of drawing simple symbols that expressed specific sounds. By stringing the symbols together and matching the sounds to the symbols, they could form a word. Then they could interchange the symbols to make different sounds and different words. If they could match a symbol to a sound, they could create an entire written language of all their sounds. This list of symbols is an alphabet.

So far, so good. This is where humanity hit a major snag. With the advent of language, humans learned how to share information that wasn't in their DNA. But humans are not born with the knowledge of language in their brains. Up until this time, every entity was born with all the instructions they needed to survive tightly encapsulated in their DNA. Humans changed the game. Human children are born with survival instructions in their DNA, like all living creatures. They are complete members of the natural world, which we call the ecosystem. At the same time, newborn children do not carry a single idea in their heads.

Let's talk about these things called ideas for a minute. Ideas are not physical things. If we cut open a human head, we would not find any ideas stored inside. That's because ideas are not physical in nature. So, how do we know ideas even exist?

Let's say you walk into a cave and see a picture of a circle with lines emanating from it. It looks like a sun, but you can't be sure. What is it? How did it get here? Why is it here? You have all kinds of questions about this picture on the wall. Can you answer any of these questions? Let's think about this.

For this drawing to appear inside this cave, a human would have to begin with the idea of the sun. Then they would form the idea of creating a picture of the sun. Then they would form more ideas about how to select a cave wall and materials and then actually produce the picture. The human who created these ideas is long dead. But the picture remains. So, what is the picture?

The picture represents the ideas of the human who created it. The ideas the human used when creating this picture exist in the picture itself. The drawing is like a fossil. An idea fossil. A snapshot of a long-ago human idea. We may not be exactly sure how it got there or what it means, but we can be sure the idea existed because the picture exists.

In nature, when a human dies, their DNA dies too. When this picture-drawing human died, their DNA died, but their ideas about the sun endured. They still exist. In the picture. Only humans can form ideas, and the ideas, once formed, can be produced in a form outside a body and then exist beyond a human lifetime.

For an idea to outlive a human, it must be stored outside their body. This is what makes humans unique. We can think, that is, create ideas; then we can produce physical representations of those ideas and store them outside our bodies so they can last beyond our lifetimes. Animals can only store information in a new generation of animals.

Remember when I said that all living entities existing 200,000 years ago represented all information in the world because they contained all the DNA in the world? Well, we can't say that anymore. Human information can now be stored outside of bodies, not just on cave walls, but in books and computers and buildings and clothing and toys and ships, and every other thing humans have produced since the inception of their evolution. Now we must say that all information on Earth includes all living entities plus all the things humans have created from their ideas.

What humans created when they began to think and record information outside their bodies is really an ecosystem of its own. It is parallel to nature's ecosystem. The world of human ideas acts like an ecosystem, but it is not composed of life forms, like the natural ecosystem. It is composed of ideas. It is an ecosystem of ideas. I call this ecosystem of ideas the "ideasphere." It is the ideasphere that makes humans utterly different from every other life form on Earth. No other creature can conjure up an idea and act on it the way a human can.

This is where we jump off the fact train. The ideasphere is a theory. A theory is something that conforms to existing facts but draws conclusions that cannot themselves be proven. I am proposing an ecosystem of ideas while fully acknowledging that ideas lack physical substance. Scientists have not yet devised a method of measuring the ideas that come from thinking, so this theory cannot yet be proven. No wonder no one has come up with this idea before!

Yet here we are, with ideas all around us. I believe that understanding the ideasphere as an ecosystem is key to human survival. Let's explore this idea of the ideasphere. I'm not asking you to accept it carte blanche, but I am asking that you read with an open mind and decide if these ideas are worth considering.

Let's start by looking at a standard-issue human baby. Our newborn baby is born with all her DNA instructions but no ideas. She is a full member of the ecosystem but is not yet a member of the ideasphere. Our baby is totally dependent on others to supply her with the resources she needs. At first, she uses the only tools she has—her fully functional DNA instructions. Among those tools is an especially effective one: crying. She cries. The baby does not have any ideas, so she cannot say "Feed me!" She can only cry to express her hunger. The baby's parent or caretaker then responds by feeding her. When she is fed, the crying stops. When she receives enough food, the messages to her brain change from "I am hungry" to "I am full," and she stops eating. The parents congratulate themselves that they fed their baby and that she might actually survive. But five minutes later, she begins to cry again. It appears to sound just like the "I am hungry" cry, but the parents know the baby has just been fed. What could it be? The parents pick up the baby and comfort her. The crying continues. The parents start singing. The baby cries even louder. The parents then lay the baby down and check her diaper. Indeed, her DNA instructions for processing waste were at work. The parents change her diaper. The baby stops crying.

The point, besides taking the opportunity to interject a humorous new-parent story, is that the human baby comes with only basic survival instructions. This condition of all DNA and no ideas does not last long. From the start, the parents and all the other people who encounter the baby insert ideas into the baby. They don't describe their actions like that, of course. They coo and sing and chat and snuggle. The baby, being human, begins to develop thoughts and ideas. Now, it will be some time before the baby can express the ideas she is learning. After all, she has not yet learned language, which is the way humans agree to communicate. After a while, the baby learns from her experiences. As time goes by, more and more ideas are deposited into her brain. It is a lifelong process, putting ideas into human minds. It continues until death. This process is what we call education.

Education is how we become members of the human community. It's how we learn to live as members of the ideasphere. It is absolutely crucial to surviving and thriving in a society composed of humans.

Keys to Understanding the ideasphere:
- Humans have huge brains.
- Humans can think in a way no other creature on Earth can.
- Human thinking is the process of creating ideas.
- Ideas are not physical.

- Humans used their cognitive abilities to create language so they could communicate. Language is a human gesture or sound that describes a commonly experienced thing.
- Language shortcuts the need to wait for cells to incorporate learning in their DNA.
- Writing is the act of storing ideas in external form.
- By producing physical representations of our ideas, humans can store them outside their bodies so they can last beyond their lifetimes.
- The ideasphere is the ecosystem of human ideas that runs parallel to the physical ecosystem.
- Humans are born without ideas.
- Education is how humans become members of the ideasphere.

Chapter 11

Human Information

Humans did not intend to build a new ecosystem, nor did we recognize we were doing so. Like all living entities, we evolved into this activity. We are the first and, so far, the only beings to inhabit the ideasphere. Like prokaryotes before us, we find ourselves on the cusp of a new ecosystem with no experience about how to live within it. From the moment we started thinking, we've been trying out all kinds of ideas to determine how we can best fit into this new ecosystem.

To learn how the ideasphere works, we must start simply and proceed step by step. We must also ground ourselves in fact at every step. As we progress, we will apply the factual concepts we discussed when we considered nonhuman life and examine whether humans in the ideasphere work the same way and, if not, how they differ.

Let's start with information. Information stored in DNA is the foundation of survival in the ecosystem. DNA stores information a cell needs, and the cell works as a unit to process the DNA's information into the energy and nutrients it needs for survival.

We can think of an idea as a bit of stored information within a human's brain. This is not an exact correlation. Ideas are not stored as discrete ideas but rather as signals in the synapses between neurons. Those signals are actual physical things. But the idea that results is not an actual physical thing. The idea is an accumulation of those signals that can be transferred outside the brain. To humans, the practical difference between the physical signals and our ideas is nil. We think of ideas as being stored inside our brains. The human body then takes those ideas and works as a unit to process them into actions. So, even though they are constructed differently, we can think of ideas and DNA as equivalent basic information units in their respective ecosystems.

DNA information has certain characteristics—it's protected and stable inside the nucleus, it's useful to the cell, and it's reliably and repeatedly copied. Now, let's see if information in the ideasphere matches up to the ecosystem.

Stability

When a person converts an idea into a physical form, let's say a book or a picture or a tool, it may or may not be stable. Remember our address book? The address book is a physical form of an idea created to keep track of your friends. If you make your address book out of easily torn paper and smearable ink, it is not in a stable format, so the information in it will probably not last long. But if your address book is made of durable paper and nonerasable ink, it might last a long time. In nature, stable information lasts; unstable information does not. We can say the same thing about information in the ideasphere. Only ideas recorded in a stable form endure. Other ideas, perhaps valuable ones that cannot be stored, are lost.

Protection

In the ecosystem, information is protected. DNA exists inside the nucleus, where it is kept separate from RNA and other proteins that might produce unintended reactions. In the ideasphere, ideas must also be protected to last. For example, the royal tombs in ancient Egypt remain intact after thousands of years because people mummified dead kings and placed them inside stone structures. However, the burial sites of millions of other nonroyal Egyptians who lived at the same time are not as easily found. Their remains were not stored as securely. Today, humans understand more about ancient Egyptian royalty than they do about ancient everyday Egyptians.

Usefulness

Information must be useful to the cell. Otherwise, it's merely data. To be information, the DNA must be able to process the data and create an instruction the cell can follow. It may be beneficial or detrimental, but what is essential is that the information can be acted upon. If you create an idea but never act on it, it is equivalent to data—not useful. It is only when you put an idea into action that it becomes useful. My book about human ideas started more than fifty years ago with thoughts about how humans worked. I added more ideas as I read the works of Darwin and Rothschild and Gould. But those ideas were totally useless to anyone else until I was able to organize my thoughts and record them outside my body first in electronic form, and later, in book form. Only now does it have the potential to become useful to others.

Usefulness of ideas, just like a DNA instruction, is subject to change. Just as the physical environment determines whether DNA is useful, the ideasphere environment determines whether an idea is useful. In the ecosystem, the environment is composed of all energy in all its forms on Earth. In an equivalent manner, the ideasphere environment is the total of all the ideas shared by humans plus all the physical representations of those ideas that humans have produced. The interaction of multiple ideas, in turn, affects the usefulness of each individual idea.

Quality

The information in the DNA of all entities is of the very highest quality. Any time DNA instructs a cell in a way that enables it to survive, its information is beneficial. If a DNA instruction causes a cell to die, not only is the DNA information unhelpful, but the cell is dead, along with its DNA. So, if you go forward like this for billions of years, the only cells left are those with beneficial information, that is, cells with DNA that can survive in their environment. As long as the entity fits into its environment, its information, that is, its DNA, is, by definition, of the highest quality for survival.

Now let's draw a parallel to the ideasphere. If the same characteristic applied to the ideasphere, we would conclude that humans who put bad ideas into action would not survive and that humans who put good ideas into action in a bad way would also die. If this were the case, the whole human race would be dead and gone by now.

Humans don't die if their ideas are bad. Because ideas have no physical presence, a bad idea can be passed on as easily and effectively as a good idea. Any idea can be passed on, regardless of quality, as long as other humans accept it. All that's needed for an idea to exist in the ideasphere is for it to be accepted and shared. There is no survival quality check on ideas like there is with cells.

Because cells live or die as a result of their actions, only cells with "good" actions survive. Ideas, however, are not tied to physical survival. A person can come up with a bad idea that others reject, and the person probably doesn't die. In fact, a person with a bad idea can continue to live on to create more ideas, good or bad, that others may or may not accept. Once an idea is accepted, however, it can take on a life of its own.

Once an idea is shared, the person who conjured up the idea can die, and the idea might still live on. This means that from the beginning of human existence, ideas that could be harmful to other humans, or other creatures, or the Earth itself could be accepted, regardless of whether they were right or wrong, good or bad. I can safely say that we have been carrying on with some very bad ideas over the years, and often, we don't know we do it. Variation in the quality of an idea in the ideasphere versus the quality of DNA in the ecosystem is one of the key differences that dramatically affects how life has unfolded on Earth.

Reliability

In the ecosystem, information must be reliably copied for a cell to survive. A cell that cannot follow an instruction the same way given the same stimulus has a greater risk of dying. As we know, in the ideasphere, ideas do not have a physical presence, and they survive by being accepted. It doesn't matter if an idea is true or good; it only matters that it be repeatable or reliable so that people accept it.

Let's use an example. Early on, the Greeks came up with elaborate stories to explain the world around them. Apollo was the god of sun and light who carried the sun across the sky in a chariot every day. This idea could not be proven, but as long as the sun came up every day, moved across the sky, and disappeared each night, the Greeks accepted this story as true. The sun's actions were repeated daily, and they were reliable, so the ideas about Apollo were accepted. Even after the people who created the ideas about Apollo died, their Apollo ideas lived on for many years. Reliability is sometimes more necessary than truth for an idea to exist. In fact, it wasn't until around the year 800 that people stopped believing in the existence of Apollo. And this occurred not because humans proved Apollo did not exist, but because Greek mythology was replaced by a different, equally unprovable religious belief, Christianity.

Truth

Let us take a little side trip to talk about truth. Two basic types of ideas exist—truth and . . . untruth. Truthful ideas are equivalent to information in the ecosystem. They are repeatable and reliable and always true under any circumstance. Like two plus two equals four. In the ideasphere, the only areas with this kind of information are the fields of science and mathematics, where even one provable instance in which an idea does not hold as true classifies the idea as untrue.

Every other idea except those known as science and math is an untruth. Not all untruths are equal. Opinion is one kind of untruth. "Blueberries are the most delicious fruit" is an opinion that is neither right nor wrong; it's a statement of personal view. An opinion cannot be proven. Opinions are ideas, just not true ones. They're still useful in the ideasphere. There's no need to prove they are true; they're not intended to be true; they are presented as ideas to consider. However, it's important to understand that they are not provably true.

Lies are also untruths. Lies are provably false. Two plus two equals five is an example. This statement is never true under any circumstance. A person can accept a lie, but again, it is important that members of the ideasphere understand that the idea they are accepting is, in fact, false.

Theories are interesting ideas. Some people don't believe in scientific theories. They argue that a theory is just a theory, so acceptance is optional. Theories are scientific facts supported by evidence, but the evidence is incomplete. Let's consider the theory of evolution. All the evidence scientists have found supports the theory of evolution. No evidence exists to refute it. But the evidence that does exist is a mere fraction of the complete fossil record. There is not enough information from Earth's past to document every step of change in a way that would completely prove evolution as fact, to make it as certain as the fact that two plus two equals four. It is in those gaps that humans turn the idea of evolution, which is supported by fact and has never been proven false, from true to uncertain.

The concept of the ideasphere is also a theory. It is rooted in fact, but because scientific efforts cannot yet measure ideas in any repeatable and reliable way, the conclusions I draw cannot be considered conclusively as fact. Darwin and his theory of evolution dealt entirely in the natural world, which is comprised only of truth and facts. Darwin had a much easier time discussing evolution than I do when discussing the ideasphere, where truth and untruth are all mixed up together.

One other untruth has played an important role in human history: beliefs. Beliefs are ideas that can neither be proved nor disproved, like the existence of Apollo, the sun god. Beliefs are not limited to religion. They're embedded in all kinds of human ideas. Let's use an airplane as an example. An aircraft is a true thing. It is based on proven mathematical and scientific principles. However, once an airplane takes off, you cannot prove that it will land safely. Airlines need to follow a lot of rules and regulations to make sure their planes land safely, but when you step onto that plane, you cannot be 100% certain of the outcome of your flight. However, most of us believe the plane will have a safe landing, or we wouldn't step on board. It is that unprovable belief that allows us to board the flight. We can see that a physical representation of an idea, like our airplane flight, can contain both truthful and untruthful elements.

The ideasphere is not as clear-cut as the ecosystem in regard to truth. The ecosystem has no untruths. The ecosystem contains only truth. Only truth and nothing else. All untruths died out long ago. We cannot say the same about our ideasphere. Our ideasphere is a jumble of truth and untruths, of facts and opinions and theories and beliefs. And it's damned difficult at times to determine which is which.

Keys to Unlocking the Ideasphere:
- Just as DNA is the basic survival information located in the cell, ideas are the basic human information stored in the synapses between brain cells.
- To endure, ideas must be recorded in a stable form, be protected, and be useful to others. An idea's usefulness can change over time.
- The ideasphere environment is the total of all shared ideas and the products made from them.
- To survive, an idea must be shared and accepted by others. The quality of the idea does not necessarily determine its acceptance.
- Ideas that are repeatable and reliable are more likely to be accepted.
- Truth is information that is repeatable and reliable and always true under any circumstance. Nature is composed entirely of truthful information.
- The ideasphere is a jumble of truth and untruth, of facts and opinions and theories and beliefs.

Chapter 12

Human Information Processing

The ecosystem and ideasphere operate in similar ways but have some profound differences in how they process information.

Let's use a story to illustrate these differences. Let's pretend you're a pie baker. How did you come to this sweet profession? Earlier in your life, you learned to speak. Then, you learned to read and write. Somewhere along the line, you learned how to read and follow recipes. You became really good at baking pies. You also learned that you didn't always need to follow a recipe, that you could combine unusual ingredients to create your own unique pies. In other words, you learned. You accumulated lots of ideas over time. You not only accumulated ideas, but you also put your ideas into action and accumulated experience. These experiences guided you to create even more ideas and more delicious pies.

Today, you are using your experience to conjure up ideas to make two kinds of pie; the first contains kiwi, butternut squash, and cayenne pepper. The second features apples, rhubarb, and roasted pecans. You bake the two pies. Your customers know that you sell your fresh pies at 4 p.m. every afternoon. By 4:10 p.m., one type of pie is sold out, each selling for $10. The other pie? By 4:30, not even one of them has sold. You spent $20 on the ingredients for all ten pies, so overall, you earned a profit of $30 (five pies sold at $10 each equals $50 in revenue, less $20 in expenses) and still have five unpurchased pies.

I think we can agree that you came up with two pie ideas, one good and one bad. The pies that sold were good because others accepted them. The pies that didn't sell were bad because nobody bought them. In the end, you had to throw out those five unappetizing pies. Losing those pies is a setback, but it's not fatal. Tomorrow, you'll make ten more pies, but now you've learned to not repeat the unappealing pie idea you had today.

A cell cannot do this. It can only follow the instructions in its DNA. Humans, however, can adjust to a harmful idea without much trouble. Humans can be proactive. They can learn from past accumulated experience and redirect their actions. Humans don't need to live with a bad result like a cell does. It is this ability to choose that is the human superpower.

Choice.

No other living entity can choose the way humans can. Choosing an idea is equivalent to selecting which DNA instructions to follow. Because ideas are not physical, humans are not as closely tied to them as cells are to their DNA instructions. For example, we've accepted the idea that eating vegetables is better for our physical health than eating pie. Yet sometimes we choose to skip the veggies and have an extra slice of pie.

Choice doesn't break the link between action and accountability, but it does delay it, sometimes so long that it's hard to connect cause and effect. If we eat pie all day, every day, and don't die, we might conclude that pies aren't bad for us at all. The ill effects on your health may not show up for months or years in the form of diabetes or heart disease. Humans can sometimes go a long way on bad choices. Humans can also go a long way on good choices. The ideasphere allows all kinds of choices to exist. It is up to humans to choose which ones to put into action.

A cell will continue to obey a bad instruction as directed by its DNA, even if it's harmful. It has no option. Humans do not have to pursue a bad idea if it is harmful. They can alter course. Humans may differ in the number of negative experiences they are willing to tolerate before implementing a different idea, but they will often alter an idea or attempt to implement a different idea before succumbing to injury or death. Choice plus experience allows humans to implement different ideas before too much damage is done.

We can see now why the ideasphere exists. It exists because it provides people with choice, and choice allows humans to avoid or delay the direct accountability that other living entities cannot escape. Deferring accountability enhances the human's chance of survival.

Let's consider how a human processes information in the ideasphere. A human is hit with an idea. For the idea to be useful, the human brain must store it in an arrangement that will allow it to be recalled later. Just as all DNA is stored in the nucleus of a cell, your ideas are stored inside your brain, but not as discrete ideas. An idea possesses no physical presence. For nonphysical ideas to exist in the brain, they are stored as physical signatures between synapses, the connection points between neurons.

Let's stop here and make a distinction that might help in further discussion. Let's call the brain of the ecosystem "the brain." And let's call the brain of the ideasphere "the mind." The mind is an accumulation of all the ideas inside the human. Since ideas are not physical, neither is the mind. It is a mental construct that helps us understand these concepts more clearly. And since we're at it, let's distinguish between humans in the ecosystem and humans in the ideasphere. Let's continue to call our physical humans "humans," but let's call our ideasphere humans "persons" or "people."

Let's say your mind conjures up the idea of having a cup of coffee. To think up this idea, you activate many neurons that travel along specific synaptic paths to your brain's processing center. It is the simultaneous activation of many neurons along specific retraced paths that is your memory. A multitude of neural pathways signaling that "coffee would be delicious right now" travel to the part of your brain where they are collected and become an idea in your mind. "Hmmm, coffee would be delicious right now."

Idea activation doesn't stop there, unless you just want to think about having a cup of coffee. You must activate more neuron paths to implement this idea. The brain and body and mind must constantly interact to actually deliver your cup of coffee. For the ideasphere to function, ideas must continuously interact with the physical brain that is part of the ecosystem. In other words, the ideasphere is totally dependent on the ecosystem for its existence. If we couldn't physically store an idea in our brain synapses, we would never be able to understand it as an idea and implement it as an action. Neurons and synapses are the translators between the two systems; they are the physical vehicles that result in a nonphysical idea. And, without the physical and nonphysical systems working in tandem, we would never get our desired cup of joe.

Unlike cells, people can learn proactively. They use their accumulated experience to create new ideas. But it's a time-consuming and energy-intensive process. In the ecosystem, a cell does not need to spend any time teaching its components how to operate—it's all there in its DNA. In the ideasphere, people are born with no ideas. In America, we use almost a quarter of an average American's lifespan teaching humans how to be proficient in the ideasphere. We expend a lot of time and energy becoming full members of the ideasphere.

Although people have choice, there really isn't a pragmatic choice to participate in the ideasphere itself. Children who grow up without human interaction don't function well at all. They are so psychologically damaged, it's difficult for them to become independent adults. Without communication, interaction and training, they typically can't get to the point where they can use their ability to think and choose and become full members of the ideasphere. All people are members of the ideasphere, whether they like it or not.

The ecosystem and the ideasphere constantly interact. Let's see how: For humans to survive in the ecosystem, they must obtain resources. To obtain resources, people must participate in the ideasphere, get their ideas accepted, put them into action, and earn resources from those actions. To put it simply, success in the ideasphere is the key to human survival in the ecosystem.

The ideasphere needs the ecosystem, but the reverse is not true. Up until 200,000 years ago, the ecosystem existed without any ideasphere, just as matter was present for billions of years before life emerged. If humans become extinct, the earth and its ecosystem will continue as if nothing happened. But the ideasphere will be dead.

That's a sobering thought for the end of a chapter.

Keys to Unlocking the Ideasphere:
- Choice is the human superpower.
- A cell can only follow its DNA instructions. A human can choose which ideas to follow.
- The ideasphere exists because it enables humans to avoid or delay the direct accountability that other living entities cannot escape. Deferring accountability enhances their chances of survival.
- Definition: brains are filled with neurons; minds are filled with ideas.
- Definition: humans are composed of cells; people are composed of ideas.
- People can learn proactively, unlike cells.
- People must be educated to be able to participate in the ideasphere.
- Success in the ideasphere is the key to human survival in the ecosystem.
- The ideasphere is totally dependent on the physical ecosystem, but the physical ecosystem is not at all dependent on the ideasphere.

Chapter 13

Characteristics of Human Life

In this chapter, we begin to contrast humans with nonhumans. All those scientific traits discussed in Chapter 4 will now provide the context and perspective we need to truly understand humans.

Information

Both the ecosystem and ideasphere are rooted in information, but the information itself is different and operates differently. DNA is physical and fixed and provides everything an entity needs to survive. Ideas are nonphysical, flexible, and can be conjured up and changed or discarded at any time without affecting a human's survival. As we can see, the fundamental bases of our systems are different.

Information processing works the same way in both systems, but the two systems operate on different levels. Living entities in the ecosystem process information to obtain resources to survive. People are more complicated. They need to conjure up ideas, put them into action, and convert acceptance of those actions into resources. The ideasphere acts as a layer that sits on top of the ecosystem. A person must successfully navigate the ideasphere to obtain the resources to survive in the ecosystem.

Building Blocks

The RNA-DNA team is the basis of all life. DNA holds all the instructions needed to ensure a cell's survival. In the ideasphere, ideas are thoughts that, when put into action, allow a person to earn the resources necessary to live. By turning ideas into actions for which others pay, people obtain resources and increase their chance of survival. We can see that accepted ideas are the foundation of success in the ideasphere and, by extension, the indirect basis of survival, just as DNA and RNA are the direct basis of survival in the ecosystem. Ideas are the basic building blocks of the ideasphere.

Fit

Entities must fit within their environment to survive. People in the ideasphere don't work quite the same way. They can actually change their environment. Let's go back to our pie story. It's 4:30 p.m. You sold all the good idea pies and have five remaining bad idea pies. You want to sell all the pies before 5 p.m., so you drop the price of the bad pies to $5. At 4:55 p.m., a customer comes in, samples a bad pie, and offers to buy all of them for $5 each. Now, your situation isn't so black and white. When the price was $10, you clearly had a set of good pie ideas and a set of bad pie ideas. When the price was $5, all the pies were good idea pies. We can venture to say that one pie idea was twice as good as the other because customers were willing to pay twice as much for it. Still, they are both good idea pies.

When you dropped the price, you created different conditions. You changed the purchasing environment of the pies and turned your bad pie idea into a good pie idea. When the conditions around the pie ideas changed, it changed the acceptance of the ideas. You changed the environment, and, as a result, you altered the acceptance of your ideas.

In the ecosystem, conditions are subject to change, but the creatures inside can't change them. A squirrel cannot instantly grow stronger legs to outrun a dog, nor can it make the dog that's chasing him smaller or slower. All the little critter can do is accept its environment as it is and use whatever abilities it currently has to avoid death, that is, to run someplace where the dog can't catch him. In the ideasphere, people can change their idea environment and affect what and how their ideas are accepted.

This does not mean the physical environment plays no part in the ideasphere. It's quite the opposite. Suppose you try to sell your pies just as a tornado is touching down. Your pies will not sell, no matter how delicious they are. You might conclude your pie ideas are bad and decide to never make those pies again, but in reality, your sales were unrelated to the quality of your pies. You just happened to operate in a physical environment that made it difficult to sell pies. Fit in the ideasphere is much more complicated than fit in the ecosystem. Not only do ideas need to be accepted, but when a person converts an idea into a physical form, the idea now also exists in the ecosystem. As such, it must comply with the ecosystem's environmental conditions as well.

Death

In the ecosystem, death serves an important purpose. Death makes sure all creatures and their DNA exit the stage, leaving only new generations to carry on with the best and most current survival instructions. Only the most fit DNA is carried forward.

Sometimes, I wish the ideasphere worked like this. It would be nice if we could kill bad ideas, but that's not easy to do. Once ideas get into a physical form—good, bad, or in-between—they can last forever.

It is possible to kill an idea—don't store it in a durable form, don't share it, and don't get others to accept it. But good luck with that. Once an idea is out and shared and accepted in the ideasphere, it's difficult to stop it from taking on a life of its own.

Let's look at death from a different perspective. When an entity produces offspring, we can say its DNA is stored in a new receptacle. People store ideas too, but we're not limited to storing them in another life form, though we do that when we have babies. We can store ideas outside our bodies in a variety of forms, for example, books, buildings, and spaceships. If we look at it this way, we can see that storage is the survival strategy in both systems. Creatures store information the only way they can, in a new body. People can store ideas outside their bodies in a zillion possible ways. As long as DNA or an idea can be stored in a sturdy new receptacle, it does not have to die.

Stored ideas can exist and evolve in the same way new generations of DNA do, but there is no guarantee that stored ideas will lead to better ideas like new generations of DNA that actually do lead to better versions than their predecessors. Ideas last as long as people accept them, regardless of how good they are. This explains why people can be so dangerous. The ideasphere's success strategy is to store a successful idea outside the human body. But a successful idea is not necessarily a good one.

Risk

Life in the ecosystem depends on obtaining enough resources to survive and procreate. Since the environment is ever-changing and full of many entities also striving to survive, the risk of death is always present and eventually catches up with every entity.

In the ideasphere, an idea may die, but it is not *required* to die like all living beings. Humans die, of course, but if they convert their ideas into a durable, fixed form, their ideas may not die at all. Once put into a durable form, ideas can not only be shared, but they can also be communicated, implemented, and modified numerous times and over a long span of time. Charles Darwin's *Origin of Species* was written in 1859. Darwin died in 1882. Yet his book was an essential source for this book written in 2024. Well stored ideas have staying power.

Resources

In the ecosystem, all living creatures need resources to survive. Humans, as members of the ecosystem, also need resources to survive. But people must also obtain ideas and put them into action to survive. If a person sits around all day and doesn't act on their ideas, it will not take long for them to die. For a person to live, they must generate ideas about how to get resources, act on those ideas, and then use the resulting resources to survive.

People are more flexible than other creatures. They are not limited to instructions specified by their DNA. People can create many ideas. Practically speaking, however, people can only conjure up new ideas based on ideas they have previously been exposed to. Like the universe, they must go step by step. There was no printing press until books existed. There were no books until written language existed. There was no written language until spoken language existed. Ideas start simply, just like all energy forms do. With time, they can grow more complex, just as all energy forms do.

Though ideas may be unlimited, not all ideas can be put into action. Because resources are scarce, the implementation of ideas is usually limited to those that are accepted by others. Let's consider our pie story again. How did your pie ideas become real? You used resources—ingredients, tools, bowls, and an oven—to bake the pie. The pie idea had no substance, but by using these physical objects, you created a physical representation of your idea, which is a . . . pie. All the items that helped you convert the pie idea into a real pie are resources.

Just as cells use resources to carry out their instructions, you used resources to put your pie idea into action. Though ideas may be unlimited, their practical application is limited by the availability of resources. People often choose which of their ideas receive resources by calculating the resources they will earn in return. In your pie-making venture, you want to earn more money than you spent making the pies. You want to earn a profit. When you earn a profit, you can not only say your pie was accepted, but you can also say your pie ideas were accepted. So, we can think of an idea as being accepted when resources are earned from it. When you earn more resources your chance of survival increases.

We know that, in the ecosystem, resource usage affects the environment. If numerous bunnies constantly eat lettuce from your garden, the resource mix of your local environment will change. There will be more bunnies and less lettuce. In the same way, when human ideas are put into action, they can affect both the ideasphere and the ecosystem. Global warming is a good example of changes that profoundly affects both systems. The idea of using coal and oil as sources of energy has produced, among other things, engines that burn coal and oil as fuel to power many of life's modern conveniences. We have now burned so much oil and coal in such a relatively short time that our planet is heating up to the point where we may not survive. We have so far not developed new energy producing ideas that are economically acceptable to people, so the ecosystem damage continues to occur. We can see that ideas alter not only the ideasphere but also our physical environment. Environments can be bent, but they never break. If we do not develop new ideas to alter these actions to reduce their environmental impact, we will lose this battle. The environment never loses.

Acceptance of an idea can also cause direct physical damage. Take war as an example. What is war but an idea? An idea that one side is right, and the other is wrong, or that one side owns stuff that the other side wants, or that one side's people look different. If that idea is accepted and turned into a decision to put resources into conquering or eliminating the "enemy," then physical damage and death result.

It is the ability to choose which ideas to implement and the willingness of many people to accept and act on the same ideas simultaneously that accelerates the speed of human change. Living entities are limited to the instructions inside their own DNA, so natural change operates much more slowly than change in the ideasphere. There is a major concern today that we humans are going to accelerate ourselves right out of existence. I believe that concern is valid.

Complexity

In the ecosystem, complexity depends on communication. Cells must communicate so they can operate in unison. To work in unison, they must be organized. More complexity requires more organization. The ideasphere works much the same way. Let's return to our pie story. Making ten pies every day requires organizational effort. You must gather the ingredients, acquire tools to prepare the pies, and have an oven to bake pies. You also must communicate with your past and future customers regarding the availability of your pies.

Let's say you now decide to open a pie store where you sell pies from 10 a.m. to 5 p.m. every day. The amount of organization required increases. Now you may need to rent a dedicated space to bake and sell the pies. You might need to make more than two types of pies or other treats besides pies, so you might need a better system for developing ideas. You will need more ovens, more bowls, and more ingredients. You might also need to hire employees to help you. Then you will need to determine how much to pay them, devise their work schedules, and decide what kind of work they will do. Your little pie idea operation has become quite complicated. And it will only be successful if you organize all these pieces to work together to implement your large-scale pie business idea. Complexity and organization go hand in hand in the ideasphere, just as they do in the ecosystem.

Self-Interest

As I mentioned, self-interest is the holy grail people often trot out to defend behavior that is harmful to others. Here is the argument: creatures in nature act to benefit their self-interest, so people should be able to act the same way. It's natural! Animals kill each other, so we can kill each other too. Eat or be eaten. Survival of the fittest. Strongest wins. Social Darwinism. I never bought into these ideas.

It's true that in the ecosystem, complex entities compete to survive. They also collaborate to survive. They also coordinate to survive. Self-interest is not built into the DNA of every entity; survival is. And there are many ways to survive. Nature exhibits no preference over which survival mechanism to pursue. Each entity performs the activities necessary for its survival, and those activities can vary. Creatures are as likely to avoid competition as they are to confront it. Collaborative cells join to make bodies and subordinate their independence in exchange for a steady stream of nourishment and a secure environment. Coordinator cells limit their entire lives to processing stimuli and directing others to do the real work of survival.

People operate differently because they have choice. Choice is the human superpower. Whenever the results of putting an idea into action cause a person harm, they can stop implementing the idea and make different choices. People can choose their ideas and actions, and as a logical extension of this concept, people can choose what self-interest means to them. There is no default self-interest mechanism for people in the ideasphere.

This opens up a wide range of ways to survive. Humans, as members of the ecosystem, require resources to survive. But people can choose their own definition of what that means. They can spend their time amassing many resources, sometimes more than they can use. Or they can amass fewer resources and spend their time on other pursuits.

Choice is the human superpower, but it is fraught with danger. We start with no ideas at birth. We are totally dependent on others putting ideas into our heads. And hoo boy, do they! All our lives, we grow up being told what we should do, what we should believe, what we should want. But all those things that we process as "shoulds" are actually choices each individual should be allowed to make for themselves. People should be allowed to choose what is important to them.

Yes, it is necessary for parents and caregivers and teachers to put ideas into the heads of babies and children to enable them to succeed in the ideasphere. But *what* is put into the head of a baby and a child makes all the difference. I wish I could say we put only the best ideas into children so they can understand how the world works and choose how best to participate in it, but we don't necessarily do that. These days, we can't even agree on how the earth was created or who won the last election. People fill children's heads with wildly different ideas, not all of which are good or helpful. Those differences have a huge effect on how we all live together.

Creatures in the ecosystem act to survive based on their genetic instructions. People in the ideasphere act on ideas they learn. Whereas entities have only one definition of self-interest, survival, humans can have many definitions of self-interest and can choose which ones to act on.

Order

If we go back to the beginning and think of the universe as filled with energy flowing in every direction, we can see that the Earth's ecosystem is merely a tiny fragment containing particular types of energy forms that consume other energy forms and convert them into offspring that are also energy forms. The ecosystem is a network held in place by resources and energy.

The ecosystem appears quite orderly because all living entities essentially grew out of the same original cell and evolved to survive. We all act the same basic way: we are born, eat resources, produce offspring with slightly different characteristics, and die. It is a circle that has continued for billions of years. The circle never stops because it is continually fueled by the energy all around us. Whatever order exists is the result of living entities committing a portion of their energy to keeping their cell members organized and operating under strict rules.

There is a limit to this order. A creature cannot control cells outside its own body; it cannot consume energy and use it to control a different body. A tiger cannot control the workings of an elephant and vice versa. If an entity cannot apply energy outside its body, it cannot produce order outside of its body either. This is why no order exists above the entity level, save for colonies. In fact, it is just the opposite. Above the individual and colony level, chaos rules. There is just energy in the form of living creatures doing whatever they can to survive as instructed by their DNA. Chaos rules in the ecosystem because living entities cannot communicate and collaborate due to their structural differences.

The ideasphere, on the other hand, is composed only of people whose unique talents have enabled them to develop sophisticated ways to communicate. If we can communicate, we can organize. If we can organize, we don't need to live in chaos. We can choose to operate differently than other entities.

People are the only creatures on this planet not forced into chaos. So why the heckadoodle do we so often choose chaos? Let's consider this in the next chapter.

These differences between nonhumans and people are important. I've summarized them in a chart to make the comparison stand out.

Ecosystem	Ideasphere	Difference
RNA-DNA building blocks	Ideas are building blocks	Ideas are not physical
Entities must fit into ecosystem environment	Humans must fit into ecosystem *and* be accepted in the ideasphere	The ideasphere is dependent on the ecosystem
Death is a survival strategy (DNA stored in new cell)	Ideas must be stored outside a human body to survive	Ideas do not necessarily die. Even bad ones.
Survival requires consumption of resources	Ideas that can be acted on and earn resources are likely to increase the chance of a human's survival	Putting ideas into action links the ideasphere to the ecosystem via resources

Resource use changes the ecosystem environment	Putting ideas into action changes both ideasphere and the ecosystem	Environment always wins regardless of the system
Complex life forms require organization	Putting complex ideas into action requires organization	Ideas are a lot more flexible than life forms when producing organization
Only surviving simple life forms grow to be more complex	Only surviving simple ideas grow to be more complex	Complex ideas can be formulated a lot faster than complex life forms
Self-interest is programmed into DNA as survival	Humans can define self-interest and choose how to act on it	Choice is the human superpower!
At the highest level of ecosystem, chaos rules	At the highest level of ideasphere, humans can choose level of organization	We can choose to live in peace. Chaos does not have to be our destiny

Keys to Unlocking the Ideasphere:
- Ideas are the basic building blocks of the Ideasphere.
- People can change the ideasphere environment through their participation.
- Storage is the survival strategy in both systems. Creatures store information in a new body. People can store ideas outside their bodies.
- All creatures of the ecosystem die. Ideas do not have to die.
- People survive by earning resources from acting on their ideas.
- Acting on ideas can change the physical environment.
- Acting on ideas can cause harm.
- Ideas can grow more complex with time, just as entities in the ecosystem do.
- People can choose what self-interest means to them. But animals in the ecosystem can only follow instructions from their DNA, which direct them toward survival.
- The ideasphere is composed only of people whose unique talents enable them to develop sophisticated ways to communicate. If we can communicate, we can organize. If we can organize, we don't need to live in chaos.
- Chaos rules in the ecosystem because living entities cannot communicate and collaborate due to their structural differences.

Chapter 14

Human Competition

I have outlined how the ecosystem and the ideasphere line up with respect to their characteristics. Although they're not exactly alike, their similarities are remarkable.

Now let's examine how our three survival mechanisms—competition, collaboration, and coordination—align. I don't think it will come as a surprise that humans, who evolved from nonhumans, use the same three mechanisms to survive. I bet you also won't be surprised that people use these tools very differently than their predecessors.

Let's start with competition. Competition is the default survival mechanism in the ecosystem. Creatures compete because it's the only way they can obtain resources. Even when they collaborate, entities don't avoid competition completely; instead, they push it up to the next organizational level. Entities compete because they can't collaborate across the ecosystem.

People roll differently. They have choice. They can choose to compete, or they can choose to collaborate. Or they can do neither. Because people can communicate, they are especially adept at collaborating. In the early days of human existence, when not many people lived on Earth, a person could eke out a living on their own. They could hunt and gather food for themselves. They could cut down trees to build a shelter. They could use natural plants and animal skins to make clothes. It might have been difficult, but they could live on their own and survive. In that case, they would be just another member of the ecosystem, competing for the resources they need. They wouldn't have to come up with ideas or have them accepted. They wouldn't have to participate in the ideasphere at all.

If a person does participate in the ideasphere, they must create ideas and put them into action in a way others accept. If we state this concept in basic economic terms, we would say they need to create a supply for an existing demand. The supply is a product or service, the physical representation of an idea. Demand is the desire for that product or service, or put another way, acceptance by others.

Why would a person choose to compete in the ideasphere? How does any survival mechanism work? Any time a choice generates more resources and increases the chances of survival, it is more likely to remain as a preferred option. People compete in the ideasphere not because they need to but because it's easier than going it alone. It's hard to forage for food and build a shelter and make your own clothes and do all the things needed to keep yourself alive. It's much easier to specialize, especially when all the members of the species can communicate and share ideas. If you are big and strong and can cut down trees and build houses but are truly awful at growing crops, maybe you can make a deal with the nearby farmers. You can build their houses in exchange for food. Wait, that sounds like collaboration. This explanation is getting confusing.

Don't worry. Collaboration and competition coexist in the ideasphere just as they do in the ecosystem. In fact, in the ideasphere, competition is actually a collaborative construct. Uh-oh. I can imagine Adam Smith rolling over in his grave. Let me explain.

If many people veer away from their rugged individualism and instead provide products and services in exchange for other products and services, a network of providers and consumers will emerge, or as economists call them, sellers and buyers. That's what we call a "market." A market is like the ecosystem that contains a giant network of providers and consumers. The difference is that in the ideasphere, participation is voluntary, or at least shaped by choice. People choose if they want to participate and, if so, how. This is the way competition in the ideasphere works. It's not required or natural at all. It's just easier than going it alone.

Competition is not a life-and-death struggle for people like it is in the ecosystem. It is a choice. Because people can communicate, share ideas, and work together to implement ideas, they can focus on the skills at which they excel. If they excel at transforming textiles into hats, for example, they are more likely to earn resources in exchange for their product, especially if others do not possess the skill and tend to walk around with burlap sacks on their heads. When a seller earns resources, they can not only purchase the goods and services they need to survive, but they can use the time they would otherwise have spent on surviving to enhance their skills. They can make top hats for formal occasions, caps with brims to shield eyes from the sun, and elaborate contraptions that seem to be required to observe famous horse races. The better the hat-making skill, the greater the differential from their customers who do not have that skill. The greater the differential, the more valuable the hats are and the more resources the person earns. Competition is not a requirement for people; it's a privilege made available to everyone who agrees to trade resources for products. Trade is a mutually beneficial exchange, which is the hallmark of collaboration.

Participation in a competitive market makes life easier for everyone who chooses to be involved. Human competition is rife with choice, unlike the ecosystem. The market is an idea, a human invention. The people who participate in the market determine its rules. They create the market environment, and participants can affect this environment merely by acting within it. If a supplier produces different products and attracts more customers, the supplier will acquire more resources and grow wealthier. If consumers prefer one product over another, the less popular one may lose its customers, thus reducing its ability to obtain resources. That producer may then go out of business.

Eighteenth-century economist Adam Smith called the multitude of choices made by people "the free market." Smith thought of the market as an entity in its own right, but really, the market is a human-created environment in which people operate. They are not trapped in it, like creatures in the ecosystem. They can change the market environment simply by choosing. The environment, that is, the market, is an accumulation of choices, so it is as ever-changing as the choices underlying it.

True freedom means living in an ecosystem where the rules exist only at the environment level. Because of their ability to communicate, people no longer experience true freedom. Over time, we have developed new ways of exchanging ideas and the products we create from them. All these creations have reduced our freedom in some way. Humans have not lived in true freedom, have not been subject to the wiles of the environment alone, for thousands and thousands of years.

In the ecosystem, we have three major levels of life: cells, organs and tissues, and bodies. Colonies exist too, but let's set them aside for a moment. In the ideasphere, we have levels equivalent to those in the ecosystem. People are equivalent to cells; institutions are equivalent to tissues and organs; and societies are equivalent to bodies. With respect to competition, only single-celled organisms and bodies compete in the ecosystem. Organs and tissues don't compete; they are arrangements of cells that exist to serve the body.

Let's talk about organs in the body in more detail. Organs don't compete at all when they exist within a body. Consider a heart organ. The heart is an arrangement of cells that work together to pump blood and keep the body alive. These cells do nothing else. The heart is essential to the body's survival. The body cannot survive without the heart, and the heart cannot survive without being included in the body where other cells in other organs perform their functions. The heart does its job for the benefit of all the other cells in the body and for the entire body itself.

Now, let's consider institutions in the ideasphere. The people in an institution join together to put a particular idea into action. Just as a single person must vie for acceptance of an idea to gain resources, so must an institution. In other words, the institutions themselves compete. This difference in how "organs" operate in the ideasphere is hugely significant. It makes them unique and powerful.

The institution's goal is to implement an idea that gains acceptance and provides the institution with resources. Let's look at the basic types of institutions in the ideasphere. Businesses convince people to accept their products or services. They call those people "customers." Religious institutions convince customers to accept their doctrines. They call their customers "believers." Nonprofit organizations convince customers to contribute money to address social problems. They call their customers "donors." Scientific organizations convince customers to understand and use scientific facts. They call their customers "doctors" and "engineers" and "chemists," to name a few.

Organs are essential players in a body. They divide up the work of living so the body can survive. In a body, the heart cells do not ingest resources on their own. The body takes in resources through the mouth, processes them into nutrients in the stomach, and then uses the heart's pumping capabilities to deliver the nutrients to all other cells in the body via the circulatory system. All the organs work together to keep the body alive.

Institutions in the ideasphere do not function this same way. Institutions are not necessarily an essential part of a society. The society does not need the institution, and the institution does not need the society.

I'm going to sidestep for a moment because I anticipate the howls of discontent. I will make an important distinction here. Societies may need the people and ideas that an institution implements, but they don't necessarily need a specific institution to implement those ideas. Other institutions may be able to perform the same function, perhaps even more efficiently. Here's a quick example: A society needs to provide energy to its citizens. It can dig up coal and burn it. It can find oil and process it into fuel and burn it. It can divide atoms, unearth geothermal power, or absorb solar energy. There are many ways to obtain energy. A society does not have to favor one particular institution that produces oil, for example. It can favor many institutions that produce oil. Or it may favor all kinds of institutions that produce all kinds of different energy. The point is that, from the society's perspective, the ideas and technology that produce energy are important, not necessarily a particular institution that provides a certain form of energy. However, from a single energy institution's perspective, its survival and ability to earn financial resources may be more important than society's preferences. You can see how conflicts between these two factions can arise. This tension between different energy producers exists today and has a dramatic effect on our society.

The link between institution and society in the ideasphere is not as tight as the link between organs and body in the ecosystem. Organs are composed of cells. The organ is a convenient and efficient grouping of cells that supports the body. The cells are what's important. In the ideasphere, the link is not nearly as tight. Institutions are composed of people—that part is similar to the ecosystem—but the institution can diverge to promote its own goals, and those goals may diverge from those of the society as a whole. Institutions can produce real benefits in a society, but they can also cause real problems. If institutions behaved more like the ecosystem, they would always work in support of the people and society around them. This is not required in the ideasphere. Institutions are free to implement their own goals without necessarily considering the effects on people or the society.

In a body, cells consume only what they need, and every cell gets what they need. If excess resources are consumed, each cell stores some of the excess. In the ideasphere, institutions earn their resources and disperse them to others as they deem necessary. Some go to the workers, some to suppliers, some to the government in the form of taxes. The owners of the institution, we call them shareholders in corporations, keep the leftover resources. Institutions generally dislike giving their money away. In fact, institutions usually do everything they can to retain as many resources as they can for themselves.

In the ecosystem, there is a downside to excess resource consumption. Generally, if a creature consumes excess resources, it almost always attempts to turn those resources into a new generation of baby creatures. If an entity continually consumes excess resources, the body must store them. It takes more and more energy for the body to store this increasing supply of excess resources. The entity's body will grow larger and become slower. Over time, it will lose its ability to compete with swifter entities and struggle to survive. Time and competition work to keep creatures fed, but not to the point where they become uncompetitive.

No such limiting force exists in the ideasphere. The owners of a company can make as many resources as they can, and they often pay no price. If the systems were exactly parallel, owners would use excess resources to create more products or more product ideas. If even more resources existed, they would then share them with all the other members of their institution or society. They don't always do that. Sometimes, institutions use excess resources to drive other competitors out of business or to pay lawmakers to create laws that benefit them.

Cells in a body are controlled by a tight neural system that limits their actions to only those that benefit the cell and the body. All cells in the body share the same DNA, so they all share the same rules. They all strive to do only one thing: survive. This arrangement does not exist in the ideasphere. All members of a society do not share the same ideas. People amass a particular subset of ideas as they grow into adults. So, by definition, not all people in a society strive for the same goals. Thinking and the superpower of choice have created a plethora of ideas. This is where the ideasphere diverges significantly from the ecosystem.

And this is where we can learn from the ecosystem. Neural systems exert strict control over their cells and organs so that they benefit both the cells and the body. But humans are thinkers and choosers; we cannot possibly live with this same level of control. But by learning from nature and adjusting for the human characteristic of choice, we might discover better ways to live.

> Keys to Unlocking the Ideasphere:
> - People can choose to compete or collaborate; entities cannot.
> - Because people can communicate, they are adept at collaboration.

- In the ideasphere, competition is actually a collaborative construct; participation is voluntary and shaped by choice.
- The ecosystem and ideasphere have equivalent levels: people are equivalent to cells; institutions are equivalent to organs; and societies are equivalent to bodies.
- In the ideasphere, institutions can compete; in the ecosystem, organs do not compete.

Chapter 15

The Effects of Human Competition

In the ecosystem, competitive pressure drives diversity, innovation, efficiency, and accountability. Let's see how competitive pressure drives people in the ideasphere. For this discussion, let's use an imaginary company that produces cigarettes. Let's start with a brief history of the industry.

We don't know who initiated the idea, but the first people to ingest tobacco smoke lived nearly 2,000 years ago. They didn't use it for enjoyment but rather for religious ceremonies. Christopher Columbus was the first documented European to learn about smoking tobacco. He brought tobacco leaves and seeds back to Europe when he returned from his expeditions, but smoking didn't become popular right away. A fellow named Jean Nicot, the French ambassador to Portugal, learned of tobacco while at his diplomatic post. He discovered that applying ground tobacco to certain tumors cured them. Tobacco was found to ease several other maladies, like headaches and stomachaches. It became common for people to grind it up and inhale it. People also chewed it. They also invented pipes so they could light the tobacco and inhale the smoke. In the early days of colonial America, colonists discovered that tobacco grew well in the region. Tobacco became one of the colonies' largest exports, and it dramatically increased the demand for slave labor in the tobacco fields.

In the early 1800s, tobacco companies began grinding tobacco and rolling it inside paper, thus dispensing with the need for pipes. Demand for these cigarettes, as they were called, grew rapidly after the Civil War, but hand-rolled cigarettes took a great deal of time to produce. In 1876, a tobacco company named Allen and Ginter offered a $75,000 prize to anyone who could invent a machine that rolled cigarettes. A young inventor named James Bonsack created such a machine and patented it in 1880. The machine was unreliable, but one manufacturer, James Buchanan Duke, bought it anyway. After some effort, the company got the machine rolling (literally) and began producing 100,000 cigarettes per day.

Soon after, intense competition followed as more manufacturers adopted the new technology. Suddenly, too many cigarettes were being produced. So companies began to market their products, even giving them out for free at public events to potential customers. They touted the "health benefits" of their product. At some point, they added stiff cards with beautiful pictures to the box and labeled them "collectibles." That idea was born out of necessity. Something was needed to keep the cigarettes from being crushed. A stiff card satisfied that need, and the beautiful picture gave the product added value.

The demand for cigarettes took off. But after about sixty years of mass consumption, the negative effects of smoking cigarettes emerged. Even people who did not smoke but lived around smokers suffered these negative effects. When stories started coming out that cigarettes were harmful to people's health, the companies did not apologize or take responsibility, change their products, or stop making their products. Instead, they went to court and spent millions of dollars to argue that it wasn't their fault their customers chose to smoke. Customers knew what they were doing. If smoking was so bad, they could have stopped. The company shouldn't pay the price when the customer chose to continue an unhealthy habit for 40 years. That argument worked for a long time.

The industry was over 100 years old before tobacco companies began losing lawsuits and started settling claims. Ironically, they didn't lose because cigarettes were deemed unhealthy. They lost because the tobacco companies knew about the addictive nature of nicotine, did not make customers aware of the fact, and intentionally enhanced the addictiveness of cigarettes to make quitting more difficult.

Yet, with all our knowledge about the harmful effects of cigarettes, tobacco companies still exist today. They still make a product that harms people. If tobacco companies were an organ in a body, and they killed or harmed other cells in the body, one of two things would happen: the neural system would put a stop to the "cigarette manufacturing cells" or the body would die.

Diversity

Okay, now that I have stated the industry history with only a slight indication of my personal bias, let's talk diversity. Diversity in the ecosystem refers to the evolution of different living forms that emerge because they can successfully respond to their environment. In the ideasphere, diversity is equivalent to putting entirely new products on the market to attract new customers. New customers that accept an idea are equivalent to new creatures that emerge in an environment. The introduction of the collectible cards was a good example. The companies needed a way to keep cigarettes from being squashed. They could have used a blank piece of cardboard. Instead, they created a new product, and they drew in new customers who may not have even wanted cigarettes but who purchased the product to obtain the cards. They created a brand-new market in which people collected and traded the cards. So, we can see that in the ideasphere, as in the ecosystem, competitive pressures can lead to diversity.

Innovation

In the ecosystem, variations in entities that result in a better chance at survival are considered innovations. Likewise, innovation in the ideasphere is the equivalent of altering products to retain your current customers and stop them from buying from your competitors. We need only go to the corner market to see how many types of cigarettes one company can produce. Low tar. High tar. Mint. Lemon. Slim. Fat. You get the idea. The products are very similar, but they are all slightly different, just like slight variations in the offspring of entities in the ecosystem. The innovations in this case are not necessarily more efficient products but rather a more efficient means of keeping customers. The variation may be just the thing to retain a customer's loyalty in an ever-changing market.

Efficiency

Efficiency means doing more with less. In the ecosystem, efficiency occurs when an entity can survive on fewer resources, obtain more resources, or produce more offspring with a given level of resources. In the ideasphere, it generally means producing the same products at a lower cost. We also call this increased productivity. The Bonsack machine was an example of how a cigarette company produced many more cigarettes with the same costs. Using the Bonsack, daily cigarette production went from a few thousand to over 100,000. With so many more products, the company could drop the price, attract many more customers, and still earn plenty of resources.

Accountability

In the ideasphere, institutions must find customers, just as creatures in the ecosystem must find food or mates with which to produce offspring. In nature, creatures have evolved a variety of ways to obtain resources, some of which are quite fascinating. A tree ocelot imitates the cry of a baby pied monkey to attract its preferred dining option of adult pied monkeys. Alligator snapping turtles wait on the bottom of a riverbed with their jaws open and wriggle a little projection in their mouth that looks like a worm, thus attracting unsuspecting fish looking for a light snack. Male peacocks advertise their sexual availability with their colorful tail feathers. Remember in nature, bodies are the only tool creatures have, so they are limited to using their bodies in innovative ways to obtain resources, but they can only display their actual physical characteristics. They are unable to describe themselves in any other way. They can't lie about their attributes. Entities don't get to lie to nature. Even if they did, nature doesn't listen. People in the ideasphere? They are not constrained by such direct accountability. People have a far wider range of possible actions and face less direct accountability for their ideas than creatures in the ecosystem.

Let's look at how our cigarette company advertises its products. Generally, companies use advertising to convince people to buy their products. "Cigarettes are good for your health" is one example. "Cigarettes are cool" is another. Some of these messages fall into the category of "provably untrue." Courts in this country have ruled that people should understand that advertising is "puffery." It's a polite way of saying something is untrue. The courts have ruled that people who hear or read advertising should understand a company is making these statements to attract customers and not necessarily to tell the truth.

In the ideasphere, a company *can* use advertising to fool people into accepting an idea that is not true, and customers may respond positively to that untrue message. If the untruth gains acceptance, it is as beneficial to the company as an accepted truth. It earns customers and resources, so it must be beneficial. From the company's perspective, false advertising may be a logical strategy, even if the product is harmful and the messages are untrue. If institutions obtain resources through guile, and they are not prevented from doing so, then they would logically conclude that guile is an acceptable practice. We can see that the level of accountability in our two systems is quite different, and much more lax in the ideasphere.

Competitors in the ideasphere and competitors in the ecosystem behave the same way. Each succeeds by using diversity, innovation, and efficiency to stay sharp and survive. But humans have choice. And choice puts a kink in human competition.

Think about what drives a company to act on an idea. Let's consider how a newly formed company behaves. When a company is young, it commits all its resources to acquiring customers. It creates products that it believes will appeal to customers and promotes these products by advertising to their potential buyers. Our young cigarette company plows its resources into survival. It makes new but related products. It innovates by making different versions of its products. It develops new techniques to lower its costs. It advertises its products with lots of puffery. These efforts attract a stream of customers who provide the company with a stream of resources.

Let us now assume our young company has done all these things and is now an older company with many resources. How does it use its resources now? Once a company has established products and possesses a customer base, its goals change. Now its goal is to keep financial resources flowing, and it can use its excess resources to prevent competitors from threatening that resource flow.

In the ecosystem, an entity cannot influence its competitive environment. It must comply or die. The ideasphere operates differently. Companies with many resources can alter their competitive environment—they can force other competitors out of the market or reduce their prices to make it difficult for new competitors to participate. Customers then purchase the lower-priced products, and the new competitor cannot earn enough revenue to cover its costs. When companies cannot earn enough money, they die, or in the ideasphere, we say they go bankrupt. Once the competitors are removed, the company again raises prices and earns more revenue.

A company can do other things too. It can use its resources to consume its competitors. Companies buy competitors and absorb their products as their own. In some cases, they may stop producing a product they absorbed so their own product sells better. In the ecosystem, entities generally do not eat their competitors. It's too risky. Instead, they use their excess resources to produce a new generation of DNA packages. In the ideasphere, resource-laden companies can and do eat their competitors.

The goal of entities in the ecosystem is to survive, and they use resources to produce offspring to achieve that goal. If the systems were exactly parallel, people would maximize the goals of the institution as expressed by their product ideas; that is, they would produce and sell as many products as possible. But people in institutions don't necessarily do this. In fact, that is often considered a bad business practice. In the ideasphere, the goal of most institutions is to obtain as much money as possible. We call this profit maximization. These institutions have prioritized obtaining resources over maximizing the spread of their product idea. In a sense, institutions have disconnected the goal of maximizing product ideas and replaced it with the goal of maximizing resources, which in nature is merely a means to achieve the goal.

Most capitalistic economists regard profit maximization as the holy grail. And it is the seed of human destruction. In my opinion.

I think it is interesting that an entire school of thought, the field of economics, has emerged to transform the act of maximizing profits into the primary goal for businesses. People who are so creative and can think up so many ideas and do so many wonderful things have somehow willingly suborned their ideas to a mere process.

In the ideasphere, money seems to hold more value than the company's ideas and products. It is the equivalent of creatures in the ecosystem eating more resources at the expense of producing offspring. If the goal of entities in the ecosystem was to maximize resources, it would not take long for the wheel of life to stop turning. If creatures in the ecosystem acted like people in the ideasphere, there would be no multicellular life to speak of, no people, and definitely no ideasphere. Life never would have gotten far enough to produce such complex beings.

I imagine a few heads just popped, so let me explain this in more detail. If we understand that our cigarette company's goal is to maximize its profits, its actions make much more sense. Presented with a choice, it always makes the choice to maximize its profits. It pays injured customers to not sue for harm caused by its products. It fights in court to avoid paying for damages its products cause. It agrees to put warning labels on its products, so government agencies won't sue them in the future. Some companies even pay government officials to make laws that benefit their operations, give them special financial advantages, or prevent others from competing with them. All these choices make sense if the goal is to maximize profits.

If a company can amass enough resources, it can game the whole competitive system. It can manipulate the environment it operates in to obtain even more resources and prevent others from competing. If creatures in the ecosystem stored excess resources this way, the wheel of life would grind to a halt. Resources would be removed from the environment and would no longer be accessible by other entities, even via competition. It is my opinion that this is happening in the ideasphere today. With most of the world's wealth stored in relatively few locations, i.e., owned by a slim minority of people, the wheel of ideas will inevitably slow down. The wheel of ideas will only be available to those with resources. Everyone else, the people with few resources, will need to comply with the ideas established by these few resource-laden individuals and institutions.

Let's talk irony. Competition did not start this way. Resource concentration flies in the face of what we believe competition and capitalism should do and were originally intended to do. The human superpower is the ability to think and choose, not to be forced to implement someone else's ideas and choices. But if resources are concentrated, the power to choose is also concentrated. It is the only logical outcome. It is the availability of resources that creates the opportunity for choice. Our current style of competition limits the superpower of choice for most people.

It wasn't always like this. In the days when Adam Smith wrote about the free market, the ideasphere was much different than it is today. In those days, the prevailing ideas were already concentrated. Kings and autocrats were the norm. Mr. Smith's writings were a revelation in new thinking. Profit maximization was a concept that made mathematical sense and acted as a roadmap to freedom. It was an idea that promoted choice. Profit maximization did not produce the same effects then that it does today. Profits were not huge. A successful business did not affect the entire market. In those days, profit maximization meant living a less arduous life. People accepted capitalism not only because it led to an easier life but also because it optimized the human superpower of choice when few other avenues of choice even existed. As time went on, people used the freedom that came with capitalism to develop more ideas. Within a few hundred years, the ideasphere was changed dramatically by the steady expansion of ideas and, relatively recently, resource concentration.

During this time of new ideas and change, the underlying concepts about capitalism did not change much. In fact, capitalism was treated with such respect that people focused on how to enhance capitalism and competition rather than noticing the effects of a changing economic environment. The success of capitalism produced a group of economists who specialized in the intricacies of this one idea, profit maximization. People specialize just as entities do in the ecosystem; that is the natural way. Some economists became profit maximization specialists, and they studied more intricate ways to maximize profits. Over time, these increasingly complex forms of competition and capitalism were implemented in a new and rapidly changing idea environment. The effect has been quite dramatic and, I would say, not wholly successful.

In 1750, resources were abundant, the air and water were clean, and ideas were rudimentary by today's standards. There were literally not enough people on Earth to affect its conditions using capitalism, or any other economic theory for that matter. We cannot say the same for today's physical environment. Today, people fight over resources that are more limited. Much of the air and water are polluted. Eight billion humans are alive today compared to approximately 800 million in 1750. The majority of monetary resources are held by a tiny minority of people. We can send information around the world in a fraction of a second, but we continue to treat the idea of capitalism as fixed and apply those fixed tenets in a fast-changing ideasphere.

I'm sure people didn't notice the subtle changes from capitalism occurring day by day, even as economists kept creating more specialized ideas that cemented profit maximization as the preferred economic goal in the ideasphere. It wasn't that people didn't notice the concentration of resources and power. It's probably more true to say that they didn't make the connection between resource concentration and capitalism. Capitalism has long been a democratizing idea, not an autocratic one. Given the association of capitalism with freedom and choice and democracy, it is quite difficult for people to overcome their implicit bias and consider that the way capitalism is being implemented today is, in fact, detrimental to choice.

I contend that it is profit maximization that is harming our superpower of choice. Let me be clear—profits are not the problem. Earning profit is equivalent to obtaining resources. This is something every person needs. The promise of profits is an effective mechanism for encouraging people to take risks and implement ideas. Profit is not the problem; it is the *maximization* of profits that produces the harm. It is the idea that a person or institution must earn profit at all costs. No law exists in the ideasphere that requires people or institutions to maximize profits. It is not an instruction that is stored inside a person's DNA that requires them to act this way. It is an idea conjured up by people that has been accepted. It has been reinforced by many smart people across many generations who have repeatedly emphasized that profit maximization is good and socially responsible.

The logical outcome of profit maximization is concentration of power. With enough resources at its disposal, an institution can keep its revenue stream flowing and prevent others from obtaining resources. This is what people do when they maximize profits. This is what they are instructed to do when they accept the idea of profit maximization. Concentration of resources leads to concentration of choice. And fewer resources lead to fewer choices. Profit maximization ultimately slows the flow of resources. It's the exact opposite of the chaotic, free-flowing ecosystem where freedom reigns and every entity must try to fit in.

So, here we are. We have established a system in which many compete, and once a few win, they do everything they can to prevent others from competing and achieving the same success. They use their resources to manipulate the economic environment to their advantage.

If a company creates harmful products like cigarettes, or dangerous products like guns, or stupid products like flying parachute outfits, it doesn't matter. If the company has enough resources, it can put those products into the ideasphere, regardless of the harm or danger or stupidity that results. The people with the most resources decide which ideas are allowed into the ideasphere and which ideas are turned into products. Those who have legitimate arguments about the harm or danger or stupidity of these ideas do not have the same influence if they can't bring the same resources to the table to fight them.

Today, with a multitude of ideas distributed across eight billion people, we have decided to use what originally was a tool to optimize human choice and turn it into a tool to achieve the exact opposite. The few with the most resources do their best to limit options. They do their best to *not* allow others the freedom to think and conjure up ideas and put them into practice. They have done everything in their power to make our ideasphere a small, limited place, when we have such potential to make a world in which we can all coexist and generate many beneficial ideas.

In capitalism, we have created a system that is natural but works against our nature. The winners of the system limit choice and the ability to think while touting their commitment to freedom. If we can just understand how competition is really working in the ideasphere, we might be able to find other ways to live together so all of us can use our power of choice.

Keys to Unlocking the Ideasphere:
- Institutions are good at acquiring many resources with no downside.
- Institutions can use excess resources to limit competition.
- In 1750, capitalism was seen as a vehicle for choice, but it has slowly transformed into a vehicle for restricting choice.
- Profit maximization ultimately leads to a concentration of resources and power.

Chapter 16

Human Collaboration

Entities in the ecosystem play only one of two roles: as a single-celled competitor or as a member of a collaborative entity. Once a cell becomes part of a multicellular entity, it remains part of that entity forever. It evolves ever after as a component of the entity, and its behavior is defined by its role as part of the entity.

Creatures in the ecosystem carry all the information they need to survive in the DNA of their cells. The DNA contains the survival information inherited from the cell's ancestors. Bees do not need to educate themselves in the ways of bees. They are born with that information encoded in their DNA. They can only draw nectar from flowers as their DNA instructs. They do not have any knowledge of flowers beyond this. They don't understand that flowers have roots or contain chlorophyll. The information embedded in their DNA is limited to only the information they need to survive.

In the ideasphere, people are capable of both competing and collaborating. The choice is not binary like it is in the ecosystem. In fact, people often blend these two mechanisms, competing in some areas and collaborating in others. In addition, people are not limited to only the instructions in their DNA. They live in the ideasphere too. They can learn. They can choose. They can create ideas. People's strength lies in their ability to communicate ideas and share them and store them outside their bodies. Compared to other creatures in the ecosystem, humans are built for collaboration.

People aren't tied to an institution the same way a cell is tied to its body. Employment is only one aspect of a person's life, not their whole life. People can choose which institutions they want to associate with. They can also perform different functions within a single organization. A mechanic can become a quality technician. A church member can become a pastor. A product designer can become a sales representative. If a person meets the requirements that an organization determines are necessary for a position, they can fill the role.

People are not limited to one institution or one choice. People are flexible. They can belong to multiple organizations at once. They can simultaneously be an employee, a member of a church, a music teacher, and a volunteer at an animal shelter.

With such flexibility, we can see that ideas can be shared and adopted by people across different fields. A robin can't go to school to learn to act like a cat. People? We can go to school and learn how to be engineers or scientists or gardeners or lawyers. We can do anything if we can learn the ideas relating to a particular area and act on them. So, we can conclude that collaboration in the ideasphere is not only optional, but it also enhances the sharing of ideas across the entire ideasphere.

Choice is the human superpower. Why would people give up the relative freedom of competition to collaborate with others and have less freedom? In the ecosystem, entities give up freedom in exchange for safety and nourishment. In the ideasphere, competition and collaboration are merely two sides of the same coin. They differ only in terms of the strength of the rules the participants must follow. In the pursuit of company profit, a collaborative institution narrows a person's actions and freedom to the performance of a specific function.

A competitive market is also a collaborative effort, but it provides a person more freedom with fewer rules. If a person believes they can profit more by competing as an individual, such as an independent bookkeeper or a plumber, for example, they may decide to implement their ideas via direct competition in a market. If a person thinks they can profit more by joining an organization that pays them a fixed wage and set hours, then they will choose to implement their ideas via collaboration. For the most part.

People don't always possess the best information to make decisions. Sometimes they don't have many choices. Sometimes they don't realize other choices exist. Sometimes other ideas are more important to them. Information is not perfectly distributed in the ideasphere, which is why education is so important. For a society to thrive, people must understand and appreciate the universe of choices available to them. Education is a critical collaborative effort made by people in societies to ensure children learn a diverse range of subjects and skills to survive and thrive in the ever-expanding ideasphere.

In the ecosystem, cells collaborate to act as organs, which together form a body. The cells act in concert but never lose their cell structure or behavior. The cells are the only ones that process information. The organs don't. The body doesn't. Only the cells. The cells are the foundation of every body.

If the ecosystem and the ideasphere were parallel, only people would be able to process information. This is, in fact, true. In the ideasphere, each person learns individually. Each person uses their knowledge and experience to create ideas. People are the only ones who can turn an idea into action. Institutions can't. The people within institutions can. Countries can't, but people within the country can. *Only* people can create and implement ideas. Just as cells are the foundation of every body, people are the foundation of every society.

In the ecosystem, organs composed of cells only operate to benefit the body. This is where the ecosystem and the ideasphere fundamentally diverge. An institution in the ideasphere can implement its own goals, separate and distinct from the goals of the society above it or the people below it. This difference has significant implications for both people and societies. Let's look at this in more detail.

People in an institution work to help the institution succeed. In our hypothetical cigarette company, the mechanic's job is to keep the machines producing cigarettes with minimal interruption. The sales representative's job is to acquire as many customers as possible. And the CEO's job is to keep everyone working in a way that maximizes profits. All the jobs are designed to earn the company the most profit possible. All good, right? Let's dive a little deeper.

Tobacco growers risk getting green tobacco sickness, also known as nicotine poisoning. Thousands of child laborers work on tobacco farms. Tobacco farming leads to deforestation, soil degradation, and agrochemical contamination. And then there are the smokers. Cigarettes contain poisons that can cause cancer in many areas of the body, including the lungs, pancreas, blood, and stomach. More than nine out of ten lung cancer deaths are attributable to smoking. Even those who don't smoke but are around cigarettes are at risk. About 7,300 Americans die each year from diseases caused by secondhand smoke.

With all this harm, cigarette companies still exist and even thrive. My point is not to diss cigarette companies. Well, maybe a little. My real point is to emphasize that the goals of an institution do not necessarily match the goals of the people it impacts or society as a whole. Cells that damage other cells of the body do not get to harm other cells with impunity. No sirree. The neural system does everything it can to put a stop to that kind of action, pronto. Such a thing doesn't necessarily happen in our ideasphere.

We know people can collaborate to form institutions. People in institutions can also collaborate across their respective institutions to pool resources and achieve common goals. This effort would be equivalent to the heart and stomach teaming up to take all the resources and leave out the rest of the organs. That does not happen in a body because all the cells share the same DNA and have no choice but to act in concert for the good of each other and the body.

Cross-institution collaboration in the ideasphere is a way for institutions to combine resources to obtain even more resources and keep them flowing in their direction. I submit a few examples, but fair warning, my biases may show.

The National Rifle Association (NRA) is an example of cross-institutional collaboration. The NRA was originally founded because soldiers in the Union Army were ineffective marksmen. The NRA taught people how to shoot and handle guns safely and often worked with the government to establish regulations to maximize the proper use of guns while minimizing their risks. Over the years, the NRA has changed its function. Influential gun manufacturers have collaborated to repurpose the NRA to promote gun ownership. This goal helps each member company maximize its profits by encouraging more gun sales. The NRA contributes significant amounts of money to lawmakers to prevent gun regulation for this very same purpose: to maximize profits from gun sales. Cross-institutional collaboration is very powerful because it amasses many resources from many profitable companies and reshapes the economic environment to benefit its participants.

Political Action Committees (PACs) are another example of cross-institutional collaboration. These are groups of people and institutions who believe in certain policies. They collect resources and direct them to candidates and lawmakers who agree to promote their causes. PACs are very powerful because they funnel significant resources to the very few decision-makers in a society to benefit their specific preferences. In essence, these few cross-institutional organizations influence decisions that affect *all* the people within that society. PACs promote the interests of the few over the interests of all.

We can see that collaboration in the ideasphere can redirect resources to benefit those with the resources. As a result, we may end up in the same place as human competition, with a small number of people with many resources influencing the entire ideasphere for their own benefit.

Mutual Benefit

In the ecosystem, collaboration is a mutually beneficial exchange. Cells trade their freedom as a single cell for a limited role and a steady supply of nourishment as a member of a collaborative entity. All cells in a body share the same DNA structure and material, but the instructions they carry out vary depending on their location in the body. People are not like cells. A company does not grow identical people in a laboratory and supply them to institutions that need them. At least not yet.

The ideasphere is a universe of ever-growing, always-changing ideas. People can only absorb and act on a subset of existing ideas. The subset of ideas they learn determines which actions they take and affects their ability to survive. In our current ideasphere, often a person's value depends on the value they bring to an institution's profit goals. It takes significant time and resources to convert a baby into a doctor, a technology specialist, or a scientist. As we know from nature, the more complicated an entity is, the fewer of them exist. A company pays more money for highly trained specialists because they are hard to make, many people value them, and few of them are available. It takes less time and training to convert a baby into a retail clerk, a barista, or a fast-food worker. As a result, more of those workers are available, and companies pay them low wages. Many companies do not care about the concepts of "sufficient resources" or "mutual benefit." They care about maximizing profits, so they pay as little as possible to obtain and keep the employees they need. Though mutual benefit is the basis of collaboration in the ecosystem, we can see that "mutual" is not necessarily part of the deal in the ideasphere.

I want to note here that companies come in all shapes and sizes. Although almost all are in business to make a profit, not every single one is tied to the idea of maximizing profits. I will say, though, as an MBA with years of business experience, that almost all large companies operate under a maximization of profit motive.

Now, back to mutual benefit. Let's return to our cigarette company again. Let's assume the company is the major employer in a small town, and most of the people who live there work at the company. In this situation, an imbalance of resources exists. The company possesses many resources, and the people depend on the company for their survival. If the company cuts wages, the workers have some options, but none of them are good. They can complain, but then they might get fired. They can uproot their family and move to another location, but that might prove risky if they don't have other employable skills. Or they may stay and accept less money because they have no other viable option. This entire problem occurs because of the resource mismatch between the company and its employees.

If an imbalance in benefit causes extreme hardship, the government might step in and enact laws to protect the under-benefited side. In this case, the government works to rebalance the benefit to be more mutual. We can conclude then that the collaborative environment in the ideasphere can be influenced by an imbalance of resources and that mutual benefit is not a default in the ideasphere like it is in the ecosystem.

Interdependence

In the ecosystem, each participating cell depends on all the other cells in the body to survive. Each cell must perform its function for the body and for the other participant cells to survive. This interdependence does not work the same way in the ideasphere. Interdependence can be temporary. People can change jobs. They can start their own companies. They can save enough to quit and not work at all. People are free to do other noninstitutional activities when they're not working. Cells in the ecosystem are not permitted such freedom. They are on the job 24 hours a day, seven days a week, for their entire lifetime. Interdependence in the ideasphere exists, but it is much less tightly connected than it is in the ecosystem.

Specialization

In the ecosystem, all cells in a body operate in a safe space. They are nourished and perform their limited functions without competition. But change is ever present, even among collaborating cells. They constantly produce variation. Entities that produce more efficient cells that benefit the body are more likely to survive. With each generation, cells become more and more specialized.

The ideasphere works the same way, but it does not have the same advantages as the ecosystem. Cells contain the accumulated experience of their ancestors in their DNA, but in our ever-expanding ideasphere, every new person who enters the system always starts at zero. A child today must learn more ideas to function in the current ideasphere than previous generations did. A child today must not only learn to read and write but must also learn how to use a cellular phone and a computer and complicated appliances. To become a specialist, people must learn significantly more information than those who came before them.

Specialization is far more difficult in the ideasphere than in the ecosystem. On the one hand, people in institutions collaborate, specialize, and advance new ideas and products at a rapid rate. But everyone starts at zero. Ironically, some people may become specialists in ideas that did not even exist at the time they were born. When education fails to provide students with the skills they need to work in fast-paced institutions, a mismatch occurs. The people who do become specialists have an advantage in obtaining employment. Those who do not obtain specialized skills face a disadvantage in finding employment. Here again, we see how important education is. It's the key to securing opportunities to specialize.

Complexity

In the ecosystem, collaboration creates complexity. Cells that collaborate can develop into complex creatures that individual cells could never become on their own. By splitting functions between different cells, they can not only perform these functions more efficiently, but they can also develop a structure that can survive in the environment as a unit of its own. Let's see if this happens in the ideasphere.

Let's return to our café from Chapter 2. , Every morning you drop by to pick up your morning cup of coffee with oat milk and a pastry that varies depending on your mood. Our café has ten employees all of which perform a variety of functions. Four baristas are busy churning out coffee drinks. One employee performs two roles; he takes coffee orders and cleans up tables and sweeps the floor when he is not taking orders. A manager in the back orders new types of coffee and plant-based milks and pastries from local suppliers. We can see that our café accomplishes tasks that you alone cannot do, or at least can't do efficiently. You would not be drinking coffee in the quantities you do if you had to grow your own coffee beans, cultivate them, roast them, and grind them before pouring them into the cool espresso machine you invented in your spare time. But our café is merely one institution in a large web of institutions across the world who collaborate to make this steaming stimulant available to you each morning. Growers and shippers and roasters and suppliers all work together in a complex network to bring coffee beans from faraway places to your local café. Bakeries with their own employees performing other functions along a different network deliver to the café that delicious almond croissant you just selected. We can go on. What is important is that we can see that functions are split among people, just as they are split among cells in a body, but people are not as tightly connected as cells in a body. Yet we *are* connected in many complex collaborative ways. So, remember that your cup of coffee is not simple at all. It is the result of a huge number of complex operations done by a huge number of people.

People are individuals. We are similar to cells in a body, but not exactly alike. We are, and will always be, individuals in both systems.

We join together to collaborate, but we can also separate and compete. We work together, but we can work alone too. We can cooperate to make complex objects, but we are separate from the objects we make. We are simple *and* complex. We are individuals and members of groups. We are a cell and a body. We are creatures of both systems.

> Keys to Unlocking the Ideasphere:
> - Humans can compete, collaborate, or do both.
> - Ideas can be shared and adopted by people across different fields.
> - Unlike entities in the ecosystem, people can change their affiliation with institutions as well as change roles within an institution.
>   o In the ideasphere, competition and collaboration differ only by the strength of the rules the participants are required to follow.
>   o Education is the key to maximizing choice.
>   o Institutions are not required to benefit people or the society.
>   o People in institutions can collaborate across their institutional lines to achieve their common goals.
>   o People may use collaboration to acquire excess resources and then use those resources to eliminate opportunities for others.
>   o Mutual benefit is not always mutual in the ideasphere. Those with excess resources dictate how the resources will be distributed in an exchange.

- Specialization is much more difficult in the ideasphere. New ideas and products advance at a rapid rate, but people always start with zero ideas.
- Collaboration produces complexity in the ideasphere, just as it does in the ecosystem.

Chapter 17

Human Coordination

We have come to the final survival mechanism, human coordination. I saved it for last because it is not only the most important in the ideasphere, but it's also the culmination of all the topics we have discussed so far.

In the ecosystem, coordination is a necessary form of collaboration. Every complex entity possesses a neural system that keeps its cells and organs working in tandem to ensure the body's survival. The neural system sets the goals of the entity, establishes the rules for how all the cells behave, and then enforces those rules. Actually, I fudged a bit. In the ecosystem, the neural system does not actually need to set the goals and rules—those already exist in the DNA of every cell. The primary job of the neural system is to enforce goals and rules that already exist.

Cells cannot proactively set goals and establish rules. The goals and rules are derived; they are inherited from long-accumulated experiences embedded inside a cell's DNA. Survival is the goal because only entities that survive exist. DNA instructions are the means by which a cell survives, that is, carries out its goal. Instructions are another name for rules.

An individual cell has a very rudimentary coordination system. For single-celled organisms, the environment acts to enforce the rules of behavior. A cell can only follow its DNA instructions. It can't adjust to any changes that come along. If conditions change and the cell is harmed, it may die. If conditions change and the cell benefits, it may survive. The DNA carries the goals and the rules, but the environment is the real coordinator. The environment enforces compliance by its mere existence.

An entity is a body composed of identical cells. Every single cell in a body shares the same DNA. So, if DNA holds the identical goals and instructions needed to survive, we can conclude that the body must also have the same goals and instructions. Therefore, the only job left for a body's neural system is to enforce the existing rules of behavior for the cells.

A cell in the ecosystem is equivalent to a person in the ideasphere. A person's ideas are equivalent to all their potential goals. A person acts on the subset of ideas that are important to them. Actions are ideas put into practice. Ideas can drive our actions. But sometimes, it works the other way. We act, and from our actions, we derive what is important to us. Like I said, humans are odd. Either way, we can see that ideas are equivalent to goals, and actions are equivalent to rules.

People can choose their goals; nonhuman entities cannot. This fundamental disparity causes coordination in the ideasphere and the ecosystem to move in very different directions. Cells can only put into action the instructions they receive from their DNA. People are born without ideas, goals, or instructions regarding how to act in the ideasphere. Humans are born only with the accumulated experience in their DNA needed for them to survive in the ecosystem.

Humans form their own goals and ideas by living. When we are born into a society or join an institution, we don't receive an automatic data dump that implants the goals of the society or institution into our heads. We don't have an auto-rule-inserter that we plug in to learn how we're supposed to act. It's up to some sort of coordinating team to create those goals and rules. Like a parent in a family. Or a CEO in a company. Or a leader in a religion.

These coordinators must do what DNA does naturally. They must determine and communicate the goals and rules to each person who joins the group. Then they must enforce the rules. We can see now why human brains are so large. The coordination job in the ideasphere is far more complex and energy expensive than it is in the ecosystem. In fact, coordinating systems at every level in the ideasphere are far more complex than their related levels in the ecosystem.

To survive, every collaborative form needs a coordination function. A family has parents. An institution has management. A country has a government. Coordination mechanisms, like all survival mechanisms, constantly evolve, even today.

People are more efficient at surviving because they exist in the ideasphere. The ideasphere enables people to think, communicate, share ideas, and store information outside their bodies. They can choose how to act. All these capabilities enable people to obtain more resources than they spend on the high cost of brain power. As long as an entity can consume more resources than it expends on bodily functions and can commit some of its excess resources to producing a new generation, the line survives. Humans included. It's just cause and effect. There's no right or wrong, good or bad. If people can obtain more resources using their ideas and actions in the ideasphere, they'll survive.

I want to veer off the subject for a moment, mostly because I think it's important. Recall that I said people choose their actions from a universe of potential goals that are their ideas.

I contend that the ideas a person chooses to act on reflect that person's morality. People can have all kinds of ideas. They can say anything, but if you really want to understand them, watch what they do. A person's behavior represents their morality. In the ecosystem, cells can't choose their behavior. They can only follow the instructions provided by their DNA. They have no choice. Therefore, it is impossible for them to have morality.

Morality is a choice. People choose to act on their most important ideas, good or bad. So morality, by definition, can be either good or bad. Each person has the power of choice, so they have the power to choose their morality.

Let's consider institutions. We can say that the goals and rules of behavior developed by an institution can be considered its morality. The goal of our hypothetical cigarette company is to maximize profits by selling cigarettes. The company's coordinating system, management, establishes rules about how employees are to perform their jobs. It provides additional rules about how employees are to treat each other at the workplace. However, the company does not create restrictions on producing unsafe products. An institution has a definition of morality related to its goals. Designating a company's morality as "good" or "bad" is irrelevant to them. The rules of behavior relate only to the goal of maximizing profit. Rules link actions to goals, but they don't necessarily assign "goodness" or "badness" to them. A company maximizes profits. A church maximizes believers. A book club maximizes the comprehension of a book. The maximization goal of any organization is its morality.

What happens when these myriad goals and actions converge or conflict between institutions? Groups are composed of people, and people are free to have their ideas and should be free to choose to act on them. In a body, the neural system allows both cells and organs to perform their functions as long as they don't hurt the other cells or the body. So, if we extend this idea to our opposing groups, we would say that the coordinating function above the institutional level would step in if people were being harmed by such an inter-institutional conflict.

The coordinating function of a society is its government. The government makes laws for the good of the people and the society. When a government sets laws, it's expressing the morality of its society. In this day and age, societies are less well defined than countries. From here on, let's use "country" as an interchangeable term for "society."

Just as people can vary in their morality, so can governments. Governments come in a wide variety of flavors. If a country's goal is to maximize its survival without concern for the well-being of its individuals, it makes laws that enforce this goal. If individuals are harmed or killed in furtherance of the country's goal, the loss is deemed acceptable. If a country's goal is to maximize the well-being of its citizens without harming others in the society, it makes laws to achieve this goal. The laws of these two nations would be very different.

Morality differs between countries because their goals vary. Even within one country, morality can evolve over time. Coordinating mechanisms of countries and their governments are important because they control the goals and rules of the country. Today, in the United States, we are undergoing an intense tussle over what the goals and rules of the country should be.

In the ecosystem, the neural system's job is to enforce the goals and rules of behavior embedded in each cell. Every cell reports its status to the brain via the neural pathways. The brain cells process these bits of information and transform them into a set of actions for certain cells. This process happens over and over and over. Coordination is the brain's only function. The brain uses this feedback loop of reporting, response, result to create accountability for every cell in the body.

Let's consider how the coordination function developed in the ideasphere from the beginning. No one knows the exact history, of course, so I'll give you a general 30,000-foot view. It's true in essence but cannot be specifically proven, so I have taken a few liberties with the details, which might make you laugh.

Early on, people banded together for mutual safety. Once people began to collaborate, the need to coordinate became apparent. Not everyone can do the same job. Someone needs to hunt, someone else needs to gather firewood, and someone else needs to make tools. If the band is to survive, the jobs must be split up, so all the survival basics are covered. The more efficiently the tasks are divided and performed, the better the survival chances are for the tribe and all its members.

At first, everyone is cooperative and happy to have found a way to ease their survival pressure through collaboration. After a while, when everyone is a little more comfortable and has a sense of where and how they fit in, some yahoo notices that the members who cook the food are a little pudgier around the middle than everyone else. Maybe the members who hunt prey have more sway when it comes to making decisions. Or the members meet another band that appears to have more food and better housing.

Time is a means by which change occurs and energy flows. Differences emerge over time. People have minds. They can observe and ponder things. They develop ideas from these observations. And because each person is unique, they conjure up a variety of ideas, some of which may conflict. The members need to decide which ideas to follow and which ideas to reject. That's where coordinators come in. They are the leaders. The deciders.

Survival is always the underlying goal, but once survival pressures are eased, people may turn their attention to other concerns. One subgroup wants to grow food instead of hunt for food. Another subgroup wants to take another tribe's possessions rather than hunt for their own. Yet another group wants to focus on the sun god to attain eternal life. People, being people, listen to these different ideas and start considering goals beyond mere survival.

How do they decide which goals to pursue? How are any ideas chosen? By acceptance. If the goal finds acceptance, it survives. So, the leaders—the coordinators—are the ones who get their ideas accepted. If enough members accept the leader's ideas, they are given permission, so to speak, to make the rules for the tribe and enforce them. Add a few generations where new tribe members are taught only about the new goal of society rather than their original purpose of survival, and you produce a unique society. Repeat the process with different tribes and different conditions over many years, and lots of unique societies spring up, each with its own set of goals, rules of behavior, and enforcement mechanisms.

Coordination systems in the ideasphere are as much a choice as competition and collaboration. And as with competition or collaboration, it doesn't have to be a good idea or a bad idea; it merely needs to be an accepted idea.

If members don't accept the goals, they may collaborate to promote their opposing ideas. They may write books and pamphlets or post their ideas on social media. Martin Luther took this route when he opposed the practice of indulgences in the Roman Catholic Church. No, he did not have a Facebook page. There is some dispute about whether he actually posted the 95 theses, his famous argument against the practice, on the doors of All Saints' Church in Wittenberg, Germany, but there is no dispute that some of his associates translated his Latin work into vernacular German and printed it in easily transferable pamphlets. The theses spread across the country in mere weeks, giving force to the split.

Sometimes people split off and become a new society with a different coordinating goal. Or sometimes they set up a sub-society within the larger society and do their best to survive. The Kurds are an ethnic group of 30 to 45 million people spread mostly across Turkey, Iran, Iraq, and Syria. The group maintains its ethnic coordination system within larger countries that have their own coordination systems.

People may also resort to violence to install a different set of coordinators. The American Revolutionary War is an example of one group, the American colonists, who rejected the coordination system under which they lived, the British monarchy, and installed a new one, a democratic republic.

At the foundation of the ideasphere is choice, the human superpower. People can choose their reasons for living together. The people with the most acceptable ideas for living together become the coordinators.

Human coordination faces the same potential problem as human collaboration and competition. If a society is successful, the coordinators can amass many resources. If the leaders of successful groups, whether they are institutions or governments, obtain a large share of the resources, problems can occur. Governments can start changing rules to benefit the leaders. CEOs can cut the wages of employees. Any time resources are concentrated in one place, the smooth operation of the mechanism can be jeopardized. Coordination mechanisms are no different.

If government leaders control vast amounts of resources, they have vast amounts of power. With excess power comes the ability to change the rules to keep themselves in power and, of course, keep the resources flowing their way. This is how governments have worked for a long time. The leaders who organized their members and obtained the most resources cemented their hold on power.

In early human history, when physical size and strength mattered, the strongest often won. They became kings or emperors or warlords. Attila the Hun is a good example. Attila was born into the Hunnic group and lived in the early fifth century, at a time when the Roman Empire was beginning to crumble. The nomadic Huns were pastoral warriors who perfected the arts of mounted archery and javelin throwing. From 434 to his death in 453, Attila led his armies all across Europe, killing people, conquering lands, and demanding gold and other resources from those he vanquished.

Once leaders obtain resources, they can then use those resources to maintain power. They change both the rules and the methods of enforcement to benefit themselves. They demand fealty. They reward their defenders with additional resources. They exile or kill their opposition. Attila did all these things. The only thing that stopped the Hunnic Empire from further expansion was Attila's death. His children fought over how to split the conquered land and were unable to use physical power to control the empire as Attila had done. The empire disintegrated due to lack of coordination.

Effective coordination, like competition or collaboration, can be subverted. Game the system to keep the resources coming. But coordination is more powerful because the coordinators have a say over the competitors and collaborators too. They make the rules *everyone* must obey. Now you can see why people fight to be the leader. It's not because they are altruistic or necessarily care about the welfare of those they lead. They may just want the resources.

Today, some countries are still led by monarchies and strongmen, but over time, people have developed other ideas about how to live together. Those older autocratic methods have been joined by democracy and communism, as well as other hybrid forms.

We are people. We can choose. We can choose to value each member of society. Or we can choose to devalue and disagree and kill each other. Or do anything in between. There is no invisible force driving us one way or the other. We drive ourselves. We set the purpose for how we live.

As humans in the ecosystem, we are subject to all of its rules. As bodies, we benefit from the strict rules that keep our cells in working order and our bodies alive. But in the ideasphere, where ideas don't have any physical structure, we can choose our goals and rules. We can choose how to compete and collaborate and coordinate. We do. People do. We choose. It's our superpower. We have not always chosen wisely.

> Keys to Unlocking the Ideasphere:
> - In the ideasphere, a person's ideas are equivalent to their goals, and their actions are equivalent to their rules.
> - People can choose their goals; nonhuman entities cannot.
> - Coordinators exist in every single individual, institution, and society:
>   o Values and goals coordinate an individual
>   o Parents coordinate families
>   o Management coordinates institutions
>   o Government coordinates a society
> - Coordinators determine and communicate the goals and rules to each person in the group.
> - The ideas a person chooses to act on represent that person's morality (author's opinion).
> - When a government sets goals and laws, it expresses the morality of its society.

- Coordinators in the ideasphere are the ones who get their ideas accepted. If enough people accept their ideas, the coordinators are given permission to make the rules and enforce them.
- Coordination systems in the ideasphere are as much a choice as competition and collaboration.
- By amassing the most resources, coordinators can skew the coordination mechanism in their favor.
- Coordination is powerful because the coordinators have a say over the competitors and collaborators too. Coordinators make the rules everyone must obey.

Chapter 18

The Nature of Human Coordination

Neural systems use very strict rules to keep their cells working together. Let's see how coordination compares in our two systems.

Disclosure

In the ecosystem, every cell reports its status to the brain via the neural system. The brain processes this information and sends a message back through the neural system to the cells that must respond. If a cell is not behaving as required, the brain issues a response to correct the behavior. This disclosure reporting is one of the most powerful tools in the neural system's toolbox.

The equivalent in the ideasphere would be what we call "disclosure laws." The census is an example of this type of law. Every ten years, the government requires each citizen to provide some basic information about themselves so it can apportion funds fairly across the country.

Today, with the cost of information processing so low, we could utilize this tool far more effectively than we currently do. Generally, our laws work in the opposite way of disclosure. We make laws, and when someone breaks them, we go after them and enforce the rules after the fact. People are accountable only if they get caught.

Neural systems don't operate this way. Or I should say that all the bodies that tried this method lost the survival game. People are not cells, so they don't need to be as tightly coordinated as cells in a body, but we might consider how some of the ecosystem survival techniques could be used successfully in the ideasphere.

Since cells have no ability to discern the quality of their actions, they must continuously send a full report of their status to the neural system. Since people and institutions are discerning, they wouldn't need to send a full report of everything they do, only those things the government decides it needs to know to keep people safe.

Let's see how disclosure laws could work in the ideasphere. Assume one of the goals of an imaginary country is to promote the general welfare of its citizens. This government decides that water pollution is a significant threat to the general welfare. So, the government mandates that every institution track the types and amounts of pollutants it discharges into the water and report them to the government on a regular basis. It's important to note that this reporting directly aligns with the country's goals. The goal of promoting general welfare is threatened by water pollution. The disclosure rule is made to detect and remove water pollution, so the health of the people is not threatened. The disclosure law is how the government determines where the threat is.

Let's see how this type of reporting affects accountability in the ideasphere. If the neural system discovered through the act of disclosure that "pollution" was occurring in the body, it would first send cells to help the cell polluters stop polluting. So, in the ideasphere, if the government receives a report that a company is polluting, it would send in people to help the company stop polluting. This is very different from our current system, which looks like this: pollute, hide, find, punish, fine.

The disclosure approach emphasizes accountability, not punishment. If a company knows it won't be punished for its infraction but instead will receive help to resolve the problem, there is a much better chance it will accept the help and won't continue to pollute. That's a win-win. The company stops its bad actions that hurt people. The society gets cleaner water. The company ends up acting in a way that does not harm people as it moves forward. No punishment is needed. Punishment only occurs if the company refuses to follow the disclosure laws or refuses to enact changes required for resolution.

Disclosure establishes efficient accountability. In a neural system, disclosure leads to the most efficient response because it can get ahead of problems before they become too big. Likewise, in the ideasphere, disclosure allows the government to reach its goals in an efficient way before they result in bad outcomes.

Nourishment

In the ecosystem, every cell is adequately nourished. If a body consumes excess resources, all cells store a share of the excess. If a body starves, all the cells share in giving up their fat and muscle stores, except for the brain, which holds on to its neurons as long as possible so it can keep the body running. This method is necessary because no choice exists in the ecosystem. This is the only way all the cells can coexist inside a body. This model evolved because it is more efficient for one organ to ingest the food and distribute it to the other cells than for each cell to nourish itself on its own. The neural system makes sure all cells are nourished so they can contribute to the body's overall well-being.

If the ideasphere was exactly parallel to the ecosystem, a society would collect all resources from every person and redistribute them to each person as needed. We don't work this way. In the ideasphere, each person is responsible for obtaining their own resources. They get a job and live off their wages, or they open a business and live off its profits.

The government takes care of the common needs of society. Common needs are things we all need but don't own individually, like roads and armies and national parks. Our government (in the United States) also provides funds for education, to low-income people, and to the elderly. These aren't common needs as much as they are priorities. We think education for all is important, so government provides it. We think it is important that low-income families have resources to make survival easier, so government provides those funds. We think elderly folks who can't work anymore should have a stable income in their later years.

We fund common needs and priorities by levying taxes. We all pay taxes, and the government applies them wherever they are needed according to their budgetary priorities. So, we can say that taxes are equivalent to nourishment in the ecosystem.

There's a big difference between the two systems. In the body, the tax rate on the ingestion system is nearly 100%, an almost total redistribution of its resources. The tax rate on all the other systems is zero. In the ideasphere, we have a multitude of taxes that have different impacts on individuals in society. As a result, our two ecosystems have very different impacts on their members. We'll talk about taxation in more detail in the next chapter.

In the ecosystem, there is no such thing as private property. The body is a publicly owned entity. In fact, the entire ecosystem is publicly owned property. You don't see squirrels yapping over who gets to hide in a tree. They don't pull out the oak tree deed and argue over who has a right to the best branch. If the dog is coming, they all clamber up the tree as quickly as possible.

Private ownership is an idea people conjured up as a way to organize themselves and distinguish one person's resources from those of another. Once people created the concept of private property, the concept of common property was forced to follow. One cannot exist without the other. Common property is property that members of a society share. Since everyone owns common property, everyone must contribute to its upkeep. Hence the need for taxation. In a sense, private property is an arbitrary idea created by the government. Irony alert. Private property is a concept invented by a public institution. Ha! It's also another reason why taxation is a much more complex undertaking in the ideasphere than in the ecosystem.

Our private property concept is not perfect. Far from it. We have a severe case of wealth inequality in our country today. Ten percent of the people in the US own 80% of the wealth. The remaining 90% owns the other 20%. At the bottom of the scale, severe poverty exists. The situation has increasingly worsened over the years. In 1989, the top 10% owned "only" 61% of all the wealth in the country. In the United States today, we cannot say that all members are getting nourished as they need. A neural system does not permit this situation to occur in a body; it would endanger the body's very survival to allow such inequality.

So, why do we let this happen in the ideasphere? We take pride in having the freedom to make our own way in life. Since people can choose to work to obtain resources, it is their responsibility to do so. If they don't, there's a general sense that they are stupid or lazy or deserve to suffer. After understanding how the ecosystem and ideasphere work, we can see this is not a fair assessment.

Every person starts at zero in the ideasphere. How they survive their first few years is critical to how they function in the ideasphere. Who bears children? Young people. Who possesses the fewest resources when they start out on their own? Young people. That's a bad combination if we want everyone to succeed in the ideasphere. We can predict what happens. Those families starting with many resources do well. Their children are likely to earn even more resources as they grow into adulthood. Families starting with few resources must contend not just with the ideasphere but also with physical survival. They have a much tougher time achieving success. If we don't nourish them well enough so they can succeed in the ideasphere, we all lose. We lose the potential ideas that all these people could have created but did not get the opportunity to do so.

We aren't as connected to our institutions or governments as cells are to their body. Cells in a body share the same goals and rules. People start with no goals or rules at all and then decide on them as they go. If we want people to be more aligned, to act in a less harmful way toward one another, or to at least understand the goals and rules of the country where they live, we need to do a much better job of educating people. Currently, we don't do this very well. We educate people in a variety of ways, but we don't really focus on the civic rules of coexistence.

Let's use the US government as an example of how coordination systems work in our current ideasphere. We live in a representative democracy, which means the people essentially rule themselves. We, as individual voters, choose our leaders.

At the foundation of our country is the Constitution. The Constitution sets the goals. Like DNA information inside the nucleus of a cell, our Constitution is sturdy. It fixes our goals. It makes them as firm as the goal of survival in a body. The Constitution provides leaders with the roadmap for making laws. The laws must always comply with the Constitution. Only, in reality, the laws and the goals don't always match up.

Our Founding Fathers set up a solid system. It works very much like the ecosystem, but it accounts for the fundamental difference in humans: choice. The Constitution sets the goals. It lays out the structure for making laws and enforcing them. The legislative branch makes the laws, that is, sets the rules that support the goals. The executive branch puts the laws into action. The judicial branch has a dual role—it determines if the laws support the Constitution and if a person's actions comply with the laws. A body in the ecosystem only needs the judicial system. The body does not need a legislative branch to make rules or an executive system to do the work because the goals and rules are embedded in the DNA. We, as members of the ideasphere, need those other branches because we aren't born with the goals and rules embedded in our minds.

It's a good, solid system, but I think we've veered off track. The actions of the branches don't always match the Constitution's goals. Sometimes laws try to modify behavior coordinators don't like rather than focus on behavior that violates the goals of the Constitution. It's as if our leaders are confused about what the goal means, or worse, leaders want to redefine the meaning of a goal stated in the Constitution so as to achieve what they want rather than what was intended.

Slavery is a good example. Slavery is just about the worst thing one person can do to another. Every single person born on this planet comes from a long line of survivors extending to the beginning of time. All people are born with the power to create ideas and make choices. This power is what makes a human a person in the ideasphere. Slavery takes the personhood away from a human. No choice. No freedom to think of their own ideas. No chance to live as a true person. It is the most reprehensible thing one person can do to another, short of murder. Yet slavery is accepted in our Constitution, the very document that aspires to secure the blessings of liberty and justice for all. The neural system in a body would never permit such a contradiction, but people do. We the people can set a goal, establish a rule to match the goal, and then enforce it, but sometimes, we just don't do it. As a result, our coordinating system can cause harm and damage and destruction.

We are at a turning point in our existence. We need our coordinating systems to make decisions that will enable us to survive what could potentially be self-induced extinction. This earth is well along the path to becoming uninhabitable to humans. I'm not worried about life; life will endure. Some creatures will survive the era of humans. They will multiply and grow on an earth irrevocably changed and damaged by our species. Life is not my concern. People are.

People are the only occupants of the ideasphere. We are the only ones who can think, act on an idea, and create structures outside our bodies, whether they be books or buildings or spaceships. We are the only ones. If we are lost, the ideasphere is lost as well.

Before humans existed, countless entities lived and died, and in doing so, altered the flow of history. Humans are unique. We are the first to have created an entirely new ecosystem. Yet we have also acted in a way that places us on the precipice of destruction. We have the ability to change our behavior so we can continue to survive and even thrive.

Right now, I'm afraid. I'm not afraid that we can't change; I am afraid that we won't.

Keys to Unlocking the Ideasphere:
- Disclosure is one of nature's most powerful coordination tools.
- Disclosure laws would require people to report behavior deemed to be societally important.
- Taxation in a society is equivalent to how bodies are nourished in an ecosystem.

- Private property is a human-derived concept that does not exist in nature.
- The US Constitution sets the country's goals. It lays out the structure for making laws and enforcing them.
  - The legislative branch makes the laws.
  - The executive branch puts the laws into action.
  - The judicial branch determines if the laws support the Constitution and whether people's actions comply with the laws.
- Our society does not work as tightly as a body. We can follow nature's example and tighten up those parts that will enhance our survival.
- People are the only inhabitants of the ideasphere.

Chapter 19

The Idealsphere

I hate it when I read a book that presents a problem or theory and then doesn't provide any solutions. So, I'm not going to do that. What follows is an explanation of how we can apply lessons from the ecosystem to our current ideasphere to build a better society, which I call the "idealsphere." First, a summary.

To understand the ideasphere, we need to first understand the ecosystem. The ecosystem has existed for billions of years. Every single nonhuman creature survives in the ecosystem by complying with rules embedded within their DNA and the conditions of their environment. That's all they do. They just live every day. They eat, they procreate, they die. Over and over and over. Together, these entities tell the story of life. None of them care about the story, not one little bit. None of them care about whether they compete or collaborate or coordinate. They only do what they have evolved to do: survive.

Humans have changed the game of life. We can think. We can ask questions. We can choose how to act. We can store those choices in forms outside our bodies. Our unique capabilities have ushered in a brand-new ecosystem: the ideasphere. Fundamental to us is the question: How do we fit into the story of life? Throughout all of history, creatures lived life without that question ever arising. Now we are here, and with us comes thought, and with thought comes questions.

It has been humanity's lifelong quest to answer this question about our place in life's story. We have been puzzling over this since the moment we began to think. Here's the ironic thing: we've answered it. At least we've mostly answered it. But we just haven't realized it yet.

To understand the story of life, we must look backward and put together the pieces of what happened before we arrived. Look around. The clues to the answer are everywhere. Astronomers have unlocked information about the universe going all the way back to the Big Bang. Chemists have revealed secrets about how matter works. Physicists have uncovered forces and how they work, and they have discovered the components inside of atoms. Biologists have learned how plants and animals operate and how life forms use DNA and RNA and the myriad of proteins and enzymes to eat and procreate.

Now, I am not saying we understand everything. Nope. This universe is too ginormous and our abilities are too limited to have perfect knowledge. Yay! Full employment for scientists! There will always be more to learn.

But limited knowledge doesn't mean we don't know enough to make sense of this world. We can piece together the story. We can not only understand the story of life, but we can also use it to improve our existence in the ideasphere. When we reach backward to uncover the secret of life, we find out the secret is not hidden at all; the answers are right in front of us.

People throughout history have done a remarkable job of collecting pieces of the answer to our fundamental question. It's time we put them together and think of this world as a holistic unit and humans as a holistic part of it. This planet has a story to tell, and we are the first beings able to fathom not just this question but the answer as well. So, let's do it. Let's act as if our ideasphere is an extension of the ecosystem, because . . . it is. Let's discover what our ideasphere would be like if we followed in the footsteps of the entities that have preceded us for billions of years. Quite successfully, I might add. Let's see what the "idealsphere" could be.

All activities in the ecosystem begin and end with cells. Cells do all the real living in the ecosystem. Complex bodies are just big, complicated packages of cells that go along for the ride. Bodies live because cells live. Cells only have one goal, and that is to survive. They have transferred this goal to their organs and bodies by virtue of sharing the same DNA, that is, their operating information. So, a complex body exists to enhance the survival chances of all its cells. By doing so, the body also enhances its own chances for survival.

Inside the body, there is organized chaos. Cells are made of matter that is a unique form of energy, and energy is always moving. Always. So, each cell is constantly active. It processes resources it receives from other cells. It performs its functions as instructed by its DNA. And it reports its status to the brain via the neural system. The neural system, along with a long history of cell collaboration, limits the cells from acting too freely. If a cell drives outside its lane, it can harm other cells or the entire body. The bodies that tried the "freedom first" method didn't survive. What exists today in complex entities is what I call organized chaos. The cells in a body are free to act in whatever way their DNA allows them, as long as they don't hurt other cells or the body.

Outside a body, it's a different story. Chaos rules. Except for ants and bees who live in colonies, all animals must fend for themselves. Some creatures do congregate in flocks or herds for mutual protection, but these are loosely organized at best. At the ecosystem level, each individual unit is responsible for taking care of its own body and, with it, the cells of its body. As I've mentioned, there is no universal union of complex entities that makes rules at this level. At this level, each entity just does what it can to survive.

Now, let's compare this to an "idealsphere." Let's define the idealsphere as a structure that best suits the life forms within it, or, as we know them, people.

In our idealsphere, people are equivalent to cells. People do all the living. Not institutions. Not governments. People. Institutions and societies are just big, complicated packages of people that go along for the ride. Did you catch the similarity between humans and cells? Bodies exist because cells exist, and societies exist because people exist.

If the goal of cells is to survive, what would be the equivalent goal of people? Trick question. People have the superpower of choice, so they don't need to limit themselves to one goal. This gets even more complicated when we add in institutions and societies. Cells transfer their survival goal upward by sharing the same DNA, but this does not happen in our ideasphere. Institutions and societies can make their own goals separate from those of the people within them.

A complex body is an all-for-one, one-for-all construct, like the Three Musketeers. If people worked the same way, this would mean that, in our idealsphere, the society would act to enhance the survival chances of all its people, and by doing so, the society would also enhance its own chances of survival.

So far, so good. Let's consider the chaos question. If a cell is free to act as long as it doesn't harm the body, the same concept should apply to people in our idealsphere. Of course. Besides, choice is the human superpower. Here's the rub: ideas and choice are chaos-makers.

People can conjure up gazillions of ideas and put any number of them into action. That's what people do, and we should let them, as long as they don't harm other people or the society. When you think about it, this is the very same rule that bodies in the ecosystem live by. The only real difference is the level of chaos. People are far more free than cells in a body, so by definition, human societies should be far more chaotic. That's okay. Ideas and choice make people into chaos machines. Let them knock themselves out and be as free as they choose, as long as they don't harm others or the greater society in the process.

Now, let's look at the other end of the ecosystem. Complex entities in the ecosystem must fend for themselves. They have only a very limited ability to communicate and collaborate with members of their own species. Entities living in colonies have developed more advanced communication capabilities, but even these fascinating abilities do not compare to the human superpower of choice. Some entities have developed mutually beneficial behaviors with other species, but these actions are not performed via communication as much as by long-accumulated experience that enhances survival. Hardly any entities practice cross-species collaboration, which leaves competition as the major driving force.

The ideasphere, on the other hand, is composed of only one species, humans, and we can all communicate. So, the idea that people must *only* compete in the broader environment is silly. Really. Silly. We can communicate and collaborate. In fact, our ability to create ideas and make choices makes collaboration our key survival mechanism. If we couldn't share ideas and collaborate with others to put those ideas into action, we wouldn't be able to survive long in the ecosystem, much less in the ideasphere. So, it is logical to conclude that mass chaos is not our fate at the top level of the ideasphere. We are all people. We can all communicate. We can all choose. So, we can just as easily choose to collaborate as to compete.

This is interesting: At the individual level of the ideasphere, people are far more chaotic than cells in the ecosystem. But at the top of the ideasphere, people have the potential to be far less chaotic than creatures in the natural ecosystem.

So, if I were to describe the underlying goal of the idealsphere, it would be this:

People ought to be free to create any idea and convert it to any action they want, as long as their actions do not harm other people or the society as a whole.

Keys to Unlocking the Ideasphere:
- We do not need to know everything to understand how humans operate.
- The "Idealsphere" is a world in which societies operate using the characteristics of the ecosystem adjusted for human choice.

- Mass chaos is not our fate at the top level of the ideasphere.
- There is one and only one commandment if we want to survive:
    People ought to be free to create any idea and convert it to any action they want, as long as their actions do not harm other people or the society as a whole.

Chapter 20

Solutions

From our discussion, we can see that our two systems line up. I have put this comparison into a handy chart that will help you understand how truly similar humans and nonhumans are.

Ecosystem Levels	Ideasphere Levels	Role
DNA	Idea	Information Holder
Genome/Brain	Mind	Makes cell/human unique
Cell	Person	Information Processor
Organ	Institution	Different goals
Body	Country/Society	Body more tightly organized
Colony	Multinational Union	Colony more tightly organized
	World Society	Not possible for ecosystem
Ecosystem	Ideasphere	PARALLEL

Since people are collaborative entities, coordination is their most important survival mechanism. Ha! What am I saying? In *every* complex body, coordination is the most important survival mechanism.

In the ecosystem, goals and rules are embedded in cells. The only job the neural system must do is keep every cell in line, and that one job takes a boatload of energy. So, how should coordination be structured in our idealsphere? We now have our goal, so that's one coordination job knocked off the list:

People ought to be free to create any idea and convert it to any action they want, as long as their actions do not harm other people or the society as a whole.

Government is what we call human coordination at the society level. To understand how governments should be organized in the idealsphere, it's helpful to start by comparing existing forms of government.

Monarchies, oligarchies, and aristocracies are types of governments where one or a small number of people rule a society for their own benefit. As with all collaborations, an exchange of benefit exists between the rulers and the people. For example, the rulers may offer protection from invasion in exchange for loyalty and taxes. In these structures, the leader sets the rules, including how the people are allowed to compete and collaborate. The benefit may be mutual, but it is rarely equal. Most of the power and resources rest with the leaders. If people play by the rules, the people can do as they please. The only power the people have is their ability to unite as a group to demand change or overthrow the leaders, so leaders usually take actions to prevent this from happening.

These sorts of coordination structures last as long as the people benefit under the rule, or they do not believe they can successfully challenge the rulers. If individual choice and the ability to live a satisfying life become too difficult, then the people may decide they have nothing to lose by removing the leadership and attempting to overthrow the rulers. The American Revolution is an example of this.

Communism is a system where a small group of leaders governs a society for the benefit of the country. In this structure, the leadership group creates an entirely collaborative society in which every individual's role is determined in order to maximize the well-being of the state. This structure is destined for failure, even more so than monarchies and oligopolies. Why? Because it is even more imbalanced than monarchies. First, this system removes the superpower of humans: choice. Without choice, a person is merely a cog in a giant wheel. This goes against the very nature of people, so the rulers must spend a lot of energy and resources keeping their citizens in line. Also, when you remove the freedom to compete, you also lose the primary impetus for diversity, innovation, efficiency, and accountability. A collaborative system can produce complexity and specialization, but without the balance of competition, government systems will grow bloated and sluggish. Competition is what keeps people sharp.

Communist leaders hold the reins of power with few constraints. What do they do with such power? Do they benefit the state? Well, that's the theory, but not always the practice. Leaders do what leaders have done from time immemorial. They obtain resources and then work to keep the resources flowing their way. Once they become rich and powerful, they have little incentive to make sure the system works for the human cogs down below. The people suffer, but since the leaders exist to serve the state, their suffering doesn't matter. They translate the "well-being of the state" into the "well-being of the leaders." With all those resources, communist leaders use the same mechanisms the monarchs and oligarchs use to keep the workers in line. Threats. Intimidation. Imprisonment. Restriction of news. Torture. Internal spying. Josef Stalin is a prime example of a Communist leader who hid his abuse of individuals under the cover of "the good of the state." During his tenure as leader of the Soviet Union, he was responsible for the deaths of nearly 20 million people through labor camps, forced collectivization, famine, and executions.

China has developed an interesting twist on communism. China has kept the goal of working toward the good of the country, but they injected competition into the economic system when they discovered collaboration alone did not work well and their people were starving. This has proven to be an interesting experiment. The Chinese people have much more freedom, well, economic freedom anyway, than they used to, but their ability to think and make choices outside their economic boundaries is still limited. I am curious to learn how China's future will unfold. The education necessary to train people to perform complex jobs does not always stay confined to those areas. Ideas flow. Educated people think and sometimes want to act more freely on their ideas. China's populace has two basic choices. Either the people grow tired of the limits on their freedom and push to exert their superpower of choice. Or the people remain satisfied with the freedoms they have and do not push against their existing constraints. In other words, how wide a lane of choice do the Chinese people want to have? I don't know the answer to this question. But I do know this view will change over time. Humans are chaos machines, after all.

Last, we come to democracy and representative republics. These constructs are most like the ideasphere. The goal of democracies is the well-being of their citizenry. In democracies, all the people have a say in all the coordinating decisions to benefit all the citizens. In republics, the people vote to elect the leaders who make the coordinating decisions that benefit all citizens. The leaders in republics determine the rules that specify not only how people can use choice but also how competition and collaboration are permitted to operate in the society. Though democracies are best matched to the ecosystem, there's a lot of variation in how they're implemented. Having the goal is not enough. To be an idealsphere, the leaders must create rules that support the goal. Not all societies do this well, not even the United States.

Let us look at the United States in more detail. Overall, the US Constitution is almost perfectly aligned with the goals of the idealsphere. Those five stated goals, as specified in the preamble, are:

"... *establish Justice, insure domestic Tranquility, provide for the common defence, promote the general Welfare, and secure the Blessings of Liberty to ourselves and our Posterity.*"

These goals are about as close to "Let people do what they want as long as they don't harm each other or the society," as one can get. Yet, some of the laws and the way they are enforced have, in fact, harmed our people and hurt our society.

To form our idealsphere, we're going to have to look beyond the goals. We need to also think about how laws should work in the idealsphere. To guide us, let's remember how coordination works in the ecosystem.

Protection

In a complex entity, the neural system is isolated from the rest of the body. The cells send information through a shielded nervous system to a shielded brain. The brain processes the messages and sends a response back through protected neural paths, telling the cells to act in a way that benefits the cells and the body.

If we devised a similar system in our idealsphere, it would work something like this: The government would be shielded from influence, allowing public servants to benefit solely from doing their job serving the people. Any outside resources, such as money, influence, or pressure from individuals or institutions, should never be allowed in. Think about it. Imagine if the heart cells sent a message to the brain that said something like, "Hey, brain-buddy, send a neural response to give me more resources than the other organs and cells. In exchange, I'll pump some extra delicious, super-rich, oxygenated blood your way. Just imagine all the great thoughts you could produce with such premium blood!" That would make an excellent Far Side cartoon. Yep. And that body would be dead. So dead.

It's hard enough for a neural system to coordinate when all the cells have the exact same goals and rules. Running a government is waaay more difficult, given that we are chaos-loving, idea-producing, change-laden people. So, we should make the coordinating effort easier by removing interference from individuals and institutions that want the government to operate for their benefit rather than the benefit of all. The ideasphere still works when people and institutions influence it; it just doesn't work very well. Our government currently operates with significant private money influence. It often works to benefit the private influencers rather to benefit *all* citizens. It is safe to say the United States is *not* an idealsphere.

As governments go, so do the elections that produce their leaders. Of course, cells in a body don't hold elections, but that would be kinda fun to see. Can you imagine little signs popping out all over your skin? "Vote for the kidney team, they're renal great!" "Vote for the skin organs, they're derm good!" Okay, bad jokes aside, cells don't choose anything, but people do. So, in the idealsphere, influence should be limited to just the people. People vote. Only people should be permitted to have a say in elections. And that say should be regulated to be fair to all voters. People should be the only ones who can donate to candidates or causes. That donation process should also be regulated so that those with excess dollars cannot "speak louder" than those with fewer dollars.

Institutions should not be allowed to play any role in elections. None. Institutions act differently than organs in a body. Institutions are free to seek their goals even when their goals differ from those of society. Institutions *should* be free to seek those goals in whatever way they want, as long as they do no harm to people and the society. But because they have this freedom, they must, by necessity, be separated from the election process and the governing process. In the idealsphere, institutions should be able to use their resources to pursue their own goals, but *not* to influence the government to act on their behalf.

Our current system allows institutions to infect both the governing and election processes. Our system works; it just doesn't work very well. Now we can understand why. Governments need to be protected from self-serving institutions. We must never confuse institutions with people. Only the Constitution and its goals should drive government actions for the good of the people.

Feedback

Prohibiting outside influence in elections and government does not mean government leaders are or should be cut off from the people and institutions they serve. Of course not. Cells constantly communicate with the neural system. Communication channels should always remain open. Communication, not resources. Government in the idealsphere should have a robust system for people and institutions to feed information back to the government regarding the effectiveness of their policies and how well they align with the goal of public well-being. Bodies in the ecosystem stay ahead of problems by getting feedback early and responding as rapidly as possible before conditions worsen. Regular communication to leaders is necessary in the idealsphere; it just shouldn't come with any demands other than the demand to comply with the goals as stated in the Constitution, that is, the good of the people.

Roles

In the ecosystem, the neural system does only one thing: enforce the rules so all cells coexist, and the body survives. In the human body, the brain accounts for only 3% of the body's mass but uses 20% of the energy a body consumes. Coordination is energy intensive. The situation is even more energy intensive in the ideasphere, where the government must make the rules as well.

A neural system does nothing but coordinate. If our idealsphere looked like a neural system, governments would make laws and enforce them. That's it. The government would not perform any of the functions needed to keep the society rolling, save rulemaking and enforcement. In the ecosystem, all other actions are the responsibility of the different organs and cells that have perfected their function over eons and eons of collaboration and competition. So, what does this mean? Education, water treatment, urban planning, road building. All kinds of activities our current governments do should be done by private individuals and industries in an idealsphere.

What, you say? Blasphemy! These roles are too important to leave to profit-seeking industrialists who care only for money. Yep. I totally agree. Let me complete the thought.

Privatizing these roles does not mean the government has no say. On the contrary. When societal goals are being carried out, governments have *all* the say. They make and enforce the rules that the private institutions must follow. And this is where their efforts should be focused.

Let's use education as an example. Instead of using its resources to do the educating, the government establishes a series of requirements about the goals of education and the ideas and information to be passed on to children so they can thrive in the ideasphere. These would be serious, comprehensive requirements that would introduce students to all the opportunities available to them in the ideasphere. Then, the government would create a comprehensive system to make sure these goals are met. In addition, the government would create a comprehensive feedback loop that would enable teachers, who are the education experts after all, to continually provide leaders with information about new and effective teaching techniques. Also, the choice of which school to attend would remain with the student, not the educational institution. Though government funds the cost of education, the student chooses which institution to attend. If more students apply to a school than there are positions available, admittance would be determined by lottery.

What would be different about private educational institutions in the idealsphere is that the goal of the education institutions is now not profit alone; it is fulfillment of society's goals *along with* profit considerations. The government hires private education institutions to meet their goals. If a company innovates new education techniques that enable them to make a profit while meeting the stated education goals, that's fine. If they break even while meeting the goals, that's fine too. If they make a profit but don't meet the goals, they are subject to review and redirection and perhaps dismissal by the government. The point is that goal fulfillment is more important than profit making.

The point of this discussion is not to pick on one industry or threaten a particular group. For the record, I think education is a most honorable profession, and our teachers don't always receive the respect or resources needed to perform their critical task. My point is to imagine how things might work in a world where we optimize our three survival mechanisms. Competition brings innovation and efficiency. Collaboration drives specialization and complexity. Coordination directs competition and collaboration to innovate efficiently while meeting its goals. These three mechanisms can work in tandem to empower people to thrive in the ideasphere.

Rules and Enforcement

Let's talk a little more about rules and enforcement. In the ideasphere, we refer to rules as laws. In the ecosystem, laws are not required. Every cell has built-in instructions that define its rules of behavior. We humans are born with no ideas, no goals, and no rules. What the neural system does naturally, we must work hard at just so everyone can coexist at a basic level. Governments can use three types of rules, or laws, to enable the ideasphere to become an idealsphere. Let's look at these rules.

Disclosure

This is the most powerful tool in the ecosystem toolbox. Every single cell in a complex body discloses its status to the neural system on a regular basis. Since cells do not have the ability to discern a good status from a bad status, they must constantly send all their information to the brain for it to sort out, process, and respond. But people in the ideasphere do have the ability to discern the quality of information. We don't need to send all our information to the government for processing. Besides, this would violate the whole "freedom to choose" aspect of living we rightfully value so much. That being said, there are times when disclosure is necessary and should be required of people and institutions.

Whenever the government identifies a goal that is needed to keep people and society safe, disclosure laws should be created and enforced. For instance, if our leaders determine water pollution is a threat to our well-being, we might create a law requiring every institution of a certain size to report data about how much and how often it pollutes the water and with what pollutants. Most businesses probably don't pollute at all, and they would be given a longer interval before they would have to report again. For those who do pollute, the government would provide assistance, just as the neural system does, to help these institutions change their polluting habits. Enforcement measures kick in only if businesses fail to report or do not participate in the harm-reducing activities. An institution may be fined or temporarily closed until improvements are made.

Can you see the difference between how disclosure works in the idealsphere and our current system? Currently, we set a standard, check on institutions to determine if they comply, and fine them when they don't. The incentive is to hide polluting activity and cheat to avoid punishment. The government spends its money chasing polluters rather than repairing the pollution problem. With idealspheric disclosure rules in place, the incentive is to report and fix the problem without punishment. If the goal is to create a cleaner environment, disclosure might be a better way to go. There are countless areas where such disclosure laws would work quite well. Workplace injuries. Police conduct. State and local corruption. Homelessness. Product defects. Discrimination. Disease outbreaks. We could use some serious collaboration just to compile a comprehensive list of societal goals that would benefit from disclosure laws.

Disclosure as a tool would have been impossible just one hundred years ago. The cost of providing information was very high in the early days of business organization. Today? Computers and information processing have made the cost of information, and therefore disclosure, extremely inexpensive. The cells that regularly send their information to the neural system use a portion of the energy they consume to do this necessary reporting. Institutions should be required to use some of their resources to perform this same function, but only for those activities deemed critical to the well-being of society's members.

Prohibited Activities

Most of our existing laws are prohibited activity laws. They outline prohibited activities that can cause harm or death. We do a decent job of making these laws, but we don't always do a good job of enforcing them. In a body, every cell is a valued member of the body's "society," and the neural system does everything it can to repair an errant cell. Only as a last resort, after all other efforts have failed, does the neural system instruct the cell to be removed from the body. For cells, this means death. For people, it can mean prison.

In our current ideasphere, we don't do "person repair" very well. Instead, we tend to toss people into prison, focus on punishment, and ignore necessary rehabilitation efforts. As a result, we lose many valuable contributions that we might have received from our fellow humans. If our body worked this way, humans would have much shorter lifespans.

In an idealsphere, government would do a much better job at repairing humans. Rehabilitation. Education. Health care. Mental health care. People engage in prohibited activities for many reasons, many of them rooted in difficult early-childhood experiences. If our idealsphere is to adhere more closely to its goals, we would make a greater effort to help people become full members of the idealsphere from early in life. This encouragement alone may prevent much of the need for future "repair work." Yes, there will always be some who break the law and are resistant to "repair." For those, prison may be the best option. But even then, prison should be a last resort, and it should be humane and provide opportunities for people to learn and reintegrate into society.

Of course, we can function in societies that throw a lot of people in jail. We do this now. I contend that this reflects a society that does not work well. It all depends on our goals. If our goal is to maximize the opportunity for each citizen to participate in society, then many societies, including ours, fail quite dramatically. If our goal is to imprison people for a wide array of offenses, some of which do not harm others, then we do a darn good job. In this case, our goals are deficient, and the ecosystem would be ashamed of us if it could feel shame.

Evaluation Laws

In the ecosystem, the neural system evaluates how to respond to the cells' reports by comparing them to the DNA rules that have long been established to maximize survival. If a cell is behaving in a way that reduces the body's chances of survival, the neural system responds. In the idealsphere, we might also benefit from a mechanism that determines when people and institutions are not acting in accordance with the goal of maximizing choice while minimizing harm to others.

Judicial systems are supposed to perform this function, but our judicial system today focuses mostly on whether an activity complies with existing laws, not necessarily with the goals of the Constitution. Our current judicial system is essential, but it only performs part of the job. We might want to consider creating a robust mechanism to make sure coordinators comply with society's goals. Our judicial systems sometimes do this, but only when a situation arises in which someone argues a law is unconstitutional. Bodies in the ecosystem do not wait around for one cell to complain about another cell's behavior. Neural systems regularly monitor behavior for compliance to the goals and act immediately to protect the cells and the body in the case of noncompliance.

If such an evaluation system were in place in the idealsphere, it would identify when the actions of government leaders violate the Constitution. It would examine the actions of participants in all branches of government to determine where the society's goals are not being met or are being violated. Let's see how this would work. Obviously, much more study and thoughtful consideration is needed to adequately cover this topic, but let me provide an overview.

Let's call this part of the coordination system the "evaluation branch." It would be at the same level as our current branches of government: the executive, legislative, and judicial. One part of the evaluation branch's job would be to assess whether a government action—that is, a law, an executive action, or a judicial ruling—complies with the goals of society as stated in the Constitution. Remember, in our idealsphere, the goal allows for optimal choice among citizens as long as they do not harm others or the society.

I want to inject an important note here. It is important to clarify the meaning of the term "harm." Just because a person doesn't like what another person does, this doesn't mean they are harmed by that other person's actions. Harm must cause significant financial, physical, or property damage to a person. Violating a person's sensibilities or feelings does not rise to the level of harm unless you are dealing with children. Children are a special case because they are not fully functional members of the ideasphere. When adults have their feelings hurt, they need to take up those issues with the individual with whom they disagree, person to person. Remember this, member of the ideasphere: everyone gets to feel how they feel and act how they want to act, as long as it does not rise to the "harm" level. So, put on your big boy or big girl pants and have an honest, respectful discussion about your differences when no actual harm is involved.

Let's address some examples of "nonharmful" behavior that some of our societal members don't like. These actions do not harm anyone else, so they should be freely allowed in our idealsphere.

Gay marriage. This doesn't affect anyone else other than the two people being married. This right should be maximized.

Voting. Choosing leaders is the fundamental action an individual takes to participate in the democratic coordinating function of the society. It connects an individual's power of choice to society's coordination function. Access to this right should be maximized and protected.

Abortion. Until a fetus is viable, it is solely dependent on its mother for survival. Since it cannot survive outside its mother, it is a "part" of the mother. As such, the mother retains the sole decision-making power regarding her pregnancy. It is her body, and what she does affects no one else. She should retain full choice regarding how to deal with her pregnancy. Her rights should be maximized.

Transgender identity. It is no one else's business whether a person chooses to be a female or male, regardless of their gender at birth. This choice affects only the person making it. The right should be maximized.

Contraception. Using contraception to prevent pregnancy affects no one other than the person choosing to use it. This right should be maximized.

Maximizing nonharmful rights is one side of the evaluation branch's coin. On the flip side are actions that do harm others and should be regulated to provide protection. The evaluation branch would weigh in on these areas as well, study the impacts of harmful activities, and instruct leaders on actions to protect others and the society.

Any time an action harms others, it must be regulated. Period. If we are all going to live together, we cannot have the legal right to harm each other. The neural system doesn't let a rogue heart cell beat up on its neighboring heart cells. Oh no. The neural system would put a stop to that sort of trouble on the double. Similarly, members of the idealsphere should put a stop to actions that are harmful to others. Let's consider some examples.

First, a note about regulation. Regulation requires serious study so that regulations actually do maximize both harm prevention and choice. Too often, government applies rules too broadly, leading to unintended consequences. This is why disclosure and information-gathering are essential aspects of the evaluation process. Regulation is necessary, but it should be limited only to preventing harm while maintaining as much choice as possible.

Okay. Onto potential areas of regulation.

Guns. Currently, the availability and use of guns harm innocent people in our society. Therefore, the availability and use of guns should be regulated.

Drugs. Some drugs used recreationally may not be harmful if ingested in limited amounts and in certain circumstances. The goal of regulation here is to allow some nonharmful use of drugs while regulating the harmful use of drugs.

Any time a human activity can be both benign and harmful, it must be regulated to protect others and the society. These regulations are difficult to create because, on the one hand, we should provide the opportunity for people to make individual choices, but on the other hand, we should regulate the conditions to minimize harm to others. It is difficult to develop appropriate solutions when dealing with activities that can be both benign and harmful. In my opinion, much work needs to be done in this area.

People do not always tolerate certain behaviors in others when they personally disagree with them. Yet the reality is that a wide variety of behaviors exist, and we all do not agree on their acceptability. Acceptability is not the crucial fulcrum for balancing regulation; preventing harm is. Wouldn't it be better for our governments to make rules that allow individuals to maximize their choices while also doing our best to minimize harm? I am sure we can come up with better solutions than our current ones for problems like prostitution and militias and social media. Using the premises of the idealsphere and our knowledge of nature's survival mechanisms, we can make our societies more livable. In Appendix 2, I discuss how we can make social media better by using the lessons provided by nature.

The evaluation branch would produce a very different outcome than our current judicial branch. When leaders are deemed to have violated the goals of the society (after full due process by the evaluation branch), they would not be thrown in jail. However, they would no longer be allowed to participate in society's coordinating function. They can still participate in the ideasphere as they choose, with this one exception: they lose their right to be a coordinator if it is proven that they have previously failed to support the goals of the society, namely the well-being of the citizenry.

Let me make one more point about the evaluation branch. Such a mechanism is not currently in the Constitution. As much as I love the Constitution as it is, this is an area that would require adjustment. Our Founding Fathers gave us the process for altering our original document. Those founders. They were the best. They understood that change is a natural part of life. Anyway, it's a heavy lift to make a change to the Constitution. An amendment to the Constitution must be approved by two-thirds of Congress and three-fourths of state legislatures, so it is not something to undertake unless we thought it was necessary. I think it is.

Nourishment

In the ecosystem, all cells share the resources that are ingested through the mouth and processed in the stomach. We eat. The whole body, every single cell, is nourished, though only one organ does the ingesting. The brain, which coordinates but does not perform any of the actual survival functions of the body, shares those resources in the same way as all the other organs and cells. Because of its important coordinating role, the neural system is fed first, but it doesn't consume more than it needs.

If by chance a human consumes so much food that their body cannot convert all of it into nutrients right away, each cell keeps a little bit of the excess. If you consume so much food that your individual cells can't store it all, your body creates storage locations to hold the excess. My location is on my hips. Sigh. Other people's locations are the stomach. Or the heart. By the way, excess nutrient storage isn't too helpful to a body.

A neural system's distribution of resources is equivalent to "taxation" in the ideasphere. The neural system uses its food energy to coordinate cell activity so both the cells and the body survive. In the same way, the government uses tax revenues for two purposes: one, to run the coordination activity, i.e., the government; and two, to distribute resources to those areas of the society that are necessary to achieve societal goals.

How taxes are levied is really important. The closest match humans have to the ecosystem is a sales tax. When we buy shampoo or a lawn mower, we must pay a certain portion of the cost as a tax to our state. Most states have this tax; a few do not. This is the best method of generating tax revenue, but the way we currently do it is backward. Only consumers pay sales taxes, so as a result, it's highly regressive. Let's say I make $20,000 per year. I spend all my income to buy stuff to survive, and my state charges a 10% sales tax. So, I paid $2,000 in taxes. Let's say another person makes $1 million per year. They spend $500,000 on stuff during the year and save the other $500,000. So, they spent $50,000 in sales tax. That's a rate of 5%. Yes, I am poorer than this other person, but I paid double the tax rate. Plus, I guarantee my life is a lot more difficult than my million-dollar neighbor's. I really could have used that extra $2,000.

This is not at all how things work in the ecosystem. First, disparity of resources does not exist. Second, each cell receives equivalent resources based on their need, and any excess is shared. Okay, we're not cells. We're humans with the ability to choose our life, so disparity of resources is going to occur when people make different choices. Of course. So, how should we handle taxation in the idealsphere where people get to choose their resource-producing path?

Today, we use income tax as our primary source of tax revenue. With income tax, we calculate our income, reduce it by expenses approved by the government, then pay a specific percentage of the net amount remaining as income tax. Let's see how this mechanism would work in the ecosystem. I hate to be so blunt about this, but if a body worked like the American tax system, it would be dead, dead, dead. Every cell and organ would do anything possible to maximize its "profits," that is, its net nutrients, after spending the energy it needs to survive. Then they would only grudgingly give a portion of their net nutrients to the neural system to do its coordination work. Or it would cheat and not send the neural system its portion at all and then make the brain spend its resources going after deadbeat cells instead of coordinating the body's activities. "Good luck to you, brain, you evil socialist Big Brother. You'll never get my resources." The brain would not be able to function in such an erratic environment. The body doesn't work this way because it's a nourishment system that doesn't work well.

The body's "taxation" efforts act more like a revenue tax. Let's imagine what the idealsphere would be like if we acted like a body. What if we charged every single person and institution a revenue tax, that is, a tax on the revenues and wages they take in? Now, the rate would be much lower than the rates charged with a traditional sales tax. Let's say we charge 1% for all revenue producers and add a graduated rate structure for really huge revenue makers. Let's say in 2021, I earn $40,000. At 1%, I would pay $400 to the government. Last year, Amazon grossed $470 billion in revenue. At a 1% tax rate, they would have paid the government $4.7 billion. Amazon actually paid only $2.1 billion in income taxes, less than half of our imaginary 1% revenue tax rate.

In the idealsphere, every earner, whether a worker or an institution, pays a portion of their revenue to the government right off the top, just like entities in the ecosystem. It's more efficient, and more fair. This method also allows people to choose how to use their resources once they pay their revenue tax. They don't have to worry if they'll receive a tax deduction by spending their funds on certain "approved" expenses. They can spend their resources on the things they choose to help their business without having to look over their shoulder.

Now, let's return to the income tax system. The ecosystem doesn't have anything like the income tax system. Any excess resources are shared among all the cells. But people are people, and they are incented by profit. People are and ought to be free to pursue profits in any way that does not harm others. However, we know accumulation of excess resources can be used to thwart the smooth workings of the ideasphere.

In the ecosystem, most entities enjoying excess resources immediately create offspring. If the equivalent existed in the ideasphere, every person and institution with excess resources would plow them back into their resource-producing efforts, thereby keeping the resources flowing throughout the system. This doesn't always happen here in the ideasphere. Resources are accumulated and often used to prevent others from participating in the ideasphere. The body would never allow the heart to make life worse for the kidneys or the stomach. No way. So, why do we allow people to do this?

We can avoid this problem by charging income taxes only on highly profitable institutions and highly paid individuals. Unlike the revenue tax, this tax rate would be set quite high. Let's consider how this might work by using an example. Let's say you run an imaginary company named Big Mamazon, and this year your net income is $35 billion on revenue of $500 billion. From 2009 to 2021, Big Mamazon had revenue of over $2 trillion and earned a net profit of about $90 billion. In the existing ideasphere, the company paid taxes of $16 billion in those 13 years. That's a tax rate of about 18% on its net income but less than 1% of its revenue. That's not much, considering it's the Big Mamazon of companies.

Now, let's throw Big Mamazon into the idealsphere. This year, the company will pay $5 billion in revenue tax on its $500 billion in revenue. This leaves the company with $30 billion in profit. How much of the profit should go back to the government to keep resources flowing and prevent Big Mamazon from using its resources to keep others from participating in the ideasphere? It's a good question. On the one hand, we want the company to be incented to continue to operate by keeping some of its profits. On the other hand, if it accumulates too many resources, it can wreak havoc on the competitive and collaborative environment for others. The income tax rate must balance these two competing goals. Maybe the tax doesn't kick in until the company has accumulated a certain level of resources, but when it does, the rate would be quite high, perhaps 75% or 80%.

This is just an example, so don't go apoplectic on me. After all, there's no such company called Big Mamazon. The point is that most small companies would not pay any income tax at all because they would never hit the accumulated profit minimum. Remember, they are already paying a revenue tax, so they are still contributing to society.

If a company amasses a huge amount of wealth from its operations, the chances are high that the resources are going to be locked up and not be available to other members of society. The goal of income taxation in the idealsphere is twofold: one, to keep the resources flowing, and two, to dilute the concentration of resources so they cannot be used to subvert the smooth working of the society's survival mechanisms.

Concentration of power is death to a society whose goal is to make sure all citizens have maximum opportunities to choose their future while minimizing harm to others. The revenue tax is the price we would all pay for participating in the society. The income tax is the vehicle for keeping resources moving in a way that maximizes human choice while preventing concentration of power.

Okay. That was a snapshot of how the coordinating system would work in the idealsphere. Let's move on to institutions.

Institutions

In the ecosystem, organs exist solely to serve the body. Organs are a group of cells that work in unison to perform a specific function. If cells could have devised a more efficient structure than using organs to make a body survive, they would have. But they didn't. Organs are the solution that cells and evolution together produced. They are complex, collaborative structures that perform in a way individual cells cannot.

Institutions in the ideasphere are both similar and dissimilar to organs in the ecosystem. Institutions are also efficient, collaborative structures that work to achieve a goal that an individual cannot do alone. The difference, of course, is that institutions strive to achieve their own goals and not necessarily the goals of the society or the people within it. Which is fine. Institutions are composed of people, and people like to choose how to act, so institutions are a perfectly adequate vehicle for making choices. If institutions are free to achieve their goals though, they should be subject to the same rules as any individual person who is free to maximize their choices: they can't harm other people, and they can't harm the society in which they operate. This is not new; it's the same rule every cell and every person must adhere to in their respective systems.

Institutions in the ideasphere come in all shapes and sizes, just like organs in the ecosystem. Any group of people joining together to achieve a goal is an institution. That's a wide net.

Collaborative institutions compete in the wider ideasphere just as multicellular entities do in the ecosystem. The major benefits of the survival mechanisms—innovation and productivity from competition, and complexity and specialization from collaboration—benefit institutions just as they benefit organs in a body. This is why institutions are so important in the ideasphere. Progress. Achievement. Technological advances. Complex ideas. These are the results of collaboration, which produce outcomes that a person on their own cannot achieve.

When excess profits skew the ideasphere environment, not only do the coordination efforts become less effective, but the collaborative and competitive mechanisms do as well. In other words, not only do individuals work less effectively, so do our institutions.

I feel the need to repeat how important profits are in our economic system. Profits are a useful feedback mechanism that indicates whether an institution is successfully meeting its goals.

The ability to make a profit is a proven incentive for people to start businesses and take risks. And people should benefit when they succeed at their risky activity of choice.

It's "profit maximization" that I have a problem with. When profits are prioritized above all else, the pressure to perform can become so intense that corners are cut. Let's say a product blows up and kills a customer. It may be cheaper to hide the problem and pay the customer's family not to sue than to change the product itself. If this option maximizes profits, the company may see this as the "right" action to take. But, if a company existed in the idealsphere, it may act differently. Let's say a company in the idealsphere must disclose information about customer fatalities in its annual report. And let's say this company is historically profitable, so it's subject to a high income tax rate on its very high profits. In this case, the incentive may shift. It might be better for the company to use some of its excess profits to fix its products. When it reports its injury and fatality information, it can also report how it has resolved the problem. And the money spent on the product fix protected some of the company's profits from taxation. Also, the likelihood of additional consumer fatalities has decreased. This is a win-win. When the "no harm" consideration is now required, the institution is incentivized to move toward the "no harm" goal.

Curbing profit maximization through targeted income taxation also curbs another problem that concentrates resources: maximizing shareholder wealth. When a company is public, it means lots of institutions, like organizations, foundations, and individuals, can buy shares. Shares are little pieces of the company. The share value is essentially equal to the sum of a company's profits over its lifetime. Let's say a company has made a profit of $1000 over its three-year lifespan and has issued 1000 shares to its investors. If we do the math and divide $1000 profit by 1000 shares, we can calculate each share to be worth $1. Let's say in the fourth year, the company makes a whopping $10,000. Now each share is worth $11 ($11,000 total income in four years divided by 1000 shares). When the company earns more profits, the value of each share rises.

Now, the problem exists because the owners of the public company, the shareholders, don't necessarily care squat about the company. They care more about the profits and the share price. The investor can sell a share and convert the proceeds into resources, so the higher the share price, the wealthier the investor becomes. The managers of the company know this. If they don't maximize profits for their "absentee owners," they may lose their jobs. This could not be a worse setup if society's goal is to keep institutions from harming others. All the pressure is focused on making a profit and nothing else.

If government puts a high tax rate on excess earnings and requires reporting to disclose how well an institution does in terms of not harming people or the society, the profit goal is modified, and so is the share price. The share price will still vary, but on a less volatile basis and more in line with how well an institution meets all its goals, not just its profit goals. The result of these policies, of course, is a reduction in wealth concentration among not just the companies but also the investors in those companies. This is significant today when wealthy people and institutions own the majority of all shares in this country.

Taxation of income at high levels is required to keep resources flowing. Tax revenues aren't kept in a government's vault and hidden away. They are injected back into the economy in areas that serve the goals of society: education, infrastructure, health care, housing. People benefiting from these resources are not only able to live and thrive and maximize their ability to choose their best future, but they also keep the resources moving in a way that maximizes the production of ideas in the ideasphere.

Concentration of resources puts pressure on democratic systems and pushes them toward oligopoly and autocracy. People who have gained many resources and the power that comes with them rarely give up their power without a fight. Once a country starts moving toward autocracy by concentrating resources and power, it can be challenging to stop the slide. If resources are widely distributed, however, many citizens participate, and opportunities are maximized. Democracies have a much better chance of succeeding when these conditions are present. As long as resources flow, participation follows. The promise of participation and profit moderation are conditions that favor democracies and republics.

The World

Okay, let's go to the highest level of the ideasphere. In the ecosystem, no coordination function exists above the entity and colony levels. All nonhumans exist as units that must fight for their own survival. They have no choice. Literally. Through many years of diversification and refinement of their own unique survival techniques, they have no ability to communicate. As a result, they are only able to collaborate in the most rudimentary of ways. They are left to survive primarily through competition.

Because we all can communicate in the ideasphere, we are capable of creating a worldwide coordination function that strives to do what any country's government strives to do: optimize choice with minimal harm to others and the global society. It is technically possible. We all function pretty much the same way. Despite our many different languages and ways of living, we can communicate. If we can communicate, we can collaborate. If we can collaborate, we can develop a global structure to solve worldwide issues. We can create one single coordination system in which we all live and strive to optimize choices while minimizing harm to each other and the global society. Possible? Yes. Likely? No. Why do you think that is?

The ecosystem moves slowly to collaborate, and so do we here in the ideasphere. Each time entities change, it takes a long period to sort out which collaborative structures thrive in the environment. People also take time to assess after they develop new collaborative structures. Tribes turned into towns. Slowly. Towns turned into cities. Slowly. Cities turned into states. Slowly. States turned into nations. Slowly. Nations have created multi-national unions. Slowly.

We have not yet created a coordinated singular structure for the world, but we haven't stopped moving in that direction either. Today, countries negotiate treaties with each other to achieve specific goals. Think of the Strategic Arms Limitation Talks/Treaty (SALT) between the Soviet Union and the United States. Countries also make broad alliances to promote trade or offer mutual protection. The North Atlantic Treaty Organization (NATO) is an example of this. The European Union is an effort that looks suspiciously like a colony in the ecosystem. Individual countries act like bees as they work together for the betterment of each country and the union. Most of the world's countries have joined to form the United Nations (UN).

The UN is the first real effort by the global community to work together in a coordinated way. It is not a worldwide government, but it seeks to provide global coordination when problems arise that affect all of us. It is reactive, much like a neural system in the ecosystem, rather than proactive. Here are the goals of the UN, paraphrased for brevity:

- Prevent war
- Uphold fundamental human rights
- Establish conditions for treaties to be maintained
- Promote social progress.

These are the actions the UN prioritizes:

- Practice tolerance
- Foster peaceful coexistence
- Unite to preserve peace
- Ensure armed force won't be used
- Promote economic achievement

Just by looking at these goals and actions, we can observe a parallel construction to the idealsphere:

People ought to be free to create any idea and convert it to any action they want, as long as their actions do not harm other people or the world as a whole.

Collaboration is always rough going at first. We make a lot of mistakes when we begin a new activity. The UN is a nascent "let's treat the world as a unit" effort. It is less than perfect. Countries with veto power enhance their self-interest rather than work to benefit the global community as a whole. Countries boycott participation when they disagree with the UN's actions.

The fact that we're making an effort to unite as one group to solve some problems is a huge evolutionary leap. We now have one place where all countries can come together to disclose issues, seek assistance, and discuss solutions. It does not carry the weight of a government that is expressly granted coordinating authority by its people. It's more loosely structured. The UN is more like a loose pack of lions than a tightly structured bee colony. But this is where we are on the evolutionary track.

That said, we do have a pressing problem today that needs more coordination than a pack of lions might provide: climate change.

We are only a few years away from the catastrophic breakdown of our planet's climate systems. We need to act to ameliorate, if not eliminate, this problem as soon as we can. Yesterday, if possible. To do that, we must collaborate and coordinate as a single unit.

The irony here is rich. People have created an ideasphere that produces ideas and structures outside our bodies. We've learned how to delay accountability or even avoid it when our actions don't turn out so well. As we have grown more complex, we've become more interconnected and more interdependent. Our actions have altered the environment in which we live and depend on for survival. We are now at an inflection point.

The two sides of humanity are meeting in a head-on collision. On one side is our ideasphere side—our idea-producing, structure-storing, accountability-averse people who want to be free to choose to live however we want. On the other side is our ecosystem side—our oxygen-breathing, moderate-temperature-seeking, clean-water-requiring, environment-dependent human bodies whose very existence is being threatened by our own ideasphere.

Here is the problem as I see it: To deal with a global catastrophic issue, we need the strength of a global coordinating mechanism to enable us to take difficult actions to eliminate our potential destruction while inflicting as little harm as possible on each world citizen and providing as many options as possible given the dire situation. We don't have such a global mechanism. But even though the UN is not ideally designed for this task, it has taken on the effort to produce treaties to mitigate the problem. The UN is doing a good job—probably the best job it can, given its structure. The quality of the UN's effort is not the key issue, however. This is a race with deadly consequences. We need to understand the effort that is required to solve this huge problem.

Can we grant the UN enough coordinating power to produce the necessary changes before catastrophe occurs? Can we optimize our chances of survival given these circumstances? I don't know the answer to this question, but I know a little better how to view the problem. It seems to me that we have three choices:

- Do nothing. The result is the inevitable destruction of most, if not all, of the human species.
- Use our current treaty approach, where we painstakingly

try to resolve the issue while some countries resist chipping in resources to solve the problem but will happily accept aid from other countries. The result is a risky, uncertain outcome for our survival.
- Temporarily authorize the UN to act as a coordination unit with greater power to deal with this problem. This means they would make rules to distribute resources from wealthier countries that cause climate change to those with fewer resources who are being harmed by climate change. They would also identify prohibited climate-harming behaviors and collaborate with countries to mitigate those behaviors with as little negative impact as possible. The result is an increased chance of survival.

Of course, different flavors of each option exist, except maybe the first one. The point is, this is a difficult problem that threatens our very survival, and the only way to deal with it is for all of us interdependent, interconnected, idea-producing people to work together to figure out a way to avert widespread harm and destruction so our global society survives.

What will we do? How will we respond? It would be one thing if we didn't have the capacity to solve this problem and, therefore, died out as a species, like all the others that went extinct before us. But this is not the case. We are people. We can think. We can produce ideas. We can discover problems. We can solve them. I would hate to see us die out as a species because we refused to solve the problem.

Keys to Unlocking the Idealsphere:
- The ecosystem and ideasphere operate in parallel, so we can use success strategies from the ecosystem as a guide in the idealsphere.
- Democracy is the human coordination structure most similar to nature. At the heart of each system is the well-being of the membership.
    - Protection: The coordinating system should be protected from outside influence.
    - Feedback: Disclosure laws enable the government to recognize and solve problems before they cause too much damage.
    - Roles: Government action should be limited to rulemaking and rule enforcement.
- Rules and Enforcement in the Idealsphere:
    - Disclosure laws should be used to identify societal problems early.
    - Prohibitive laws should focus first on rehabilitation.
    - Evaluation laws should be used to determine compliance with constitutional goals.
- Regulation is required for any activity that can harm others.
- Any action that does not harm others should be allowed.
- Revenue taxes are most closely related to successful nourishment systems in nature.
- Income taxes should be used only to prevent resource accumulation by the wealthiest institutions or members.

- Institutions should be free to pursue their goals as long as they do not harm people.
- Regulation and taxation can counteract the harmful effects of profit maximization.
- People do not have a global coordination system, but we have global problems that we all experience. Climate change is the most critical global problem.
- The United Nations is a nascent effort used to confront world problems.
- People must determine how to work together to solve our global problems or risk self-extinction.

Chapter 21

Next . . .

Here we are, living in an imperfect ideasphere. If we continue on our current path, we face a real risk that we won't survive. But the changes required to transform our society into an idealsphere seem daunting at best. I don't disagree. So, we'd best get started.

Change is slow. We need to go step by step. We need to take the first steps. As we proceed, the actions we need to take to produce the idealsphere will change. As people adapt to a new way of living, governments will need to respond by reevaluating priorities and redistributing resources in new ways. As we continually evolve toward an idealsphere, our actions will also evolve. Life will get better. Our chance of survival will improve. But it will not be easy, given our current starting point. Nevertheless, it is imperative that we start, no matter how difficult the task.

If we do nothing, life will go on. But humans may not. And when we exit the stage of life, we will take the ideasphere with us. Evolution, working the way it does, may never again produce an ideasphere that operates like this one.

We can change history. We now have these ideas about the ideasphere. They exist apart from the human body that conjured them up. As long as they can be accepted and shared and acted on, they can be refined to better ensure human survival. That's where you come in.

To travel from here to there, from our present status to a healthy future, from our current ideasphere to the idealsphere, it will take all of us doing our part to rethink how we exist in our interdependent world. It is up to each of us to decide whether to put these ideas into action. How? That's a fair question.

Since people do all the living and thinking in the ideasphere, people are the only ones who can make the changes needed to create the idealsphere. It is people who will need to harness the power of institutions to redirect them to maximize freedom and minimize harm. It is people who will need to be elected to office to make and implement laws that will maximize choice and minimize harm. It is people who will live every day of their lives, raising their children, interacting with friends, playing and volunteering, and, well . . . just living, in a way that maximizes choice and minimizes harm.

We, as individuals, can start living this way. Today. I can personally attest to the vastly improved quality of life that comes with this mindset. Using this one guideline as my North Star—maximize choice, minimize harm—I have found I can sort out most conflicts with clarity and without angst. So, just by living in our own personal idealsphere, we can vastly improve our own experience of living. And by interacting with others using this mindset, we can spread the positive benefits of the idealsphere.

The next step in the process is to collaborate with other people to spread the positive effects of living in an idealsphere.

Many of you are experts in your field. You know the detailed inner workings of your area of expertise. You are the leaders in your professional arena. Using the ideas and tools of the natural world and the concepts of the idealsphere, you can apply your knowledge to find new ways of working in your field that maximize choice and minimize harm. We have a lot of problems in our country and in our world. I think if you view these issues using the perspective of the idealsphere, you might come up with some very efficient and effective solutions. Then tell the world about them. Write a book. Make a podcast. Give a TED talk. Share your ideas!

Don't stop there. If you find solutions and you believe in them, widen your collaborative net. Start an institution to put your ideas into action. Become a public servant where you can act on these ideas. Run for office with the goal of seeing your ideas become law. You experts will do a much better job of coming up with solutions and conveying them than I ever could.

I developed the theory of the ideasphere because I can think broadly across many fields but not deeply into any one of them. The world needs your expertise that looks deeply into the details of particular fields. We need your knowledge applied with the same level of respect that the cells in a body give to each other and the body itself. We need you to put ideas into action that enable humans to thrive.

If we are to survive for any length of time, if we are to have a future in which our children and grandchildren can survive and thrive, we must align our ideas and actions in a way that fits the world we live in. The creatures of the ecosystem have provided the roadmap. Our minds have given us the means to read the map. It is now time to go down the road and make a better world. Remember . . .

People ought to be free to create any idea and convert it to any action they want, as long as their actions do not harm other people or the society as a whole.

Thanks for reading.

Appendix 1

A Few More Details About RNA And DNA

Recall that early Earth was loaded with lipids, carbohydrates, amino acids, and nucleic acids. This appendix goes into more detail about how DNA and RNA actually work. You don't need to understand it to grasp the concept of the ideasphere, but it is a good way to show how the step-by-step path nature takes can cause very surprising results.

Nucleic acids played an instrumental role in the development of life. In the early days, many types of nucleic acids existed, but only two survive today—ribonucleic acid and deoxyribonucleic acid. We know them as RNA and DNA. Both of these nucleic acids contain the same components, but they differ in structure and behavior.

RNA is a single-strand molecule. Ribose sugar and phosphate molecules bond together to form a single string, and a nitrogen base hangs off each ribose sugar molecule. It looks like a ladder cut in half down the middle of each rung. A single sugar-phosphate-nitrogen base combination represents a single RNA molecule. One end of the nitrogen base is held in place by the sugar bond, but the other end (the half rung of the ladder) hangs loose and is highly reactive. When RNA runs around loose in water, the nitrogen base tries to react with anything it can. If the nitrogen base attracts another nitrogen base, the two form a tight bond that tears away from the sugar-phosphate ladder. The joined nitrogen bases form proteins, which now swim around looking for things to do. A weird thing about RNA that turns out to be very important is that the nitrogen base can only react with one matching nitrogen base. Scientists call the matching molecule the complementary base.

The sugar-phosphate molecules that attach to the nitrogen base can join together in long strings to form the rail of the RNA ladder. Each RNA molecule performs a specific function, so the entire RNA strand performs a whole set of functions that occur one right after another. Some produce proteins, and some make enzymes, a type of molecule that can start a chemical reaction. During Earth's early years, a ton of different RNA strands formed to do all sorts of things.

DNA contains the same basic molecules as RNA, but it contains a different sugar, and this difference is significant. DNA uses deoxyribose sugar, which is a sugar molecule that possesses one less oxygen molecule than ribose. The deoxyribose sugar and phosphate bond like they do in RNA to make the rail of the ladder, but the nitrogen base hanging off the deoxyribose sugar is much more tightly bound to the sugar than in RNA. So, when the nitrogen base hanging in the middle attracts another nitrogen base, it clings to that nitrogen base rather than being torn from the side rail as it does in RNA. Compared to RNA, DNA looks like a complete ladder. The rails are still made of sugar and phosphate, but the sugar is now deoxyribose instead of ribose, and the rungs in the middle are tightly joined. The full ladder shape is significantly more stable than the half ladder shape of the RNA. If the DNA strand is long enough, it twists around in what scientists call a double helix. The twisted formation makes DNA even more stable. But DNA shares the same limitation that RNA does: its nitrogen bases can only react with its complementary bases.

You would think such a limitation would be a disadvantage with a new planet full of all kinds of particles swimming around trying to survive. Instead, it turned out to be a huge advantage. Can you guess why?

Let's say a small RNA strand with three nitrogen bases is innocently swimming around in the ocean when it encounters a bunch of single RNA molecules. Being reactive, the strand immediately reacts with its complements. Now you have a double ladder of two RNA strands, with each half-strand being the exact opposite of the other. When those two strands split, as they do in RNA because it is highly reactive, we have one original strand and one opposite or complement strand. If those strands swim around and pick up their complements and split again, we now get four strands—the original strand, two complements, and a copy of the original.

That was the key thing—RNA could copy itself. Sure, it was indirect and took a few steps, but RNA was able to produce an exact copy of its original strand. This was the key to life. Or to be more precise, the limitation of bonding to only one specific molecule was the key to life. When RNA collides with other particles, only one specific result can ever occur. The original can *only* make a complementary strand. The complementary strand can *only* make an exact replica of the original RNA strand. It takes a couple of steps, but it always happens the same way. So, not only can RNA copy itself, but it can do so repeatedly. If enough of the right material is hanging around, RNA can make countless copies of itself.

Even DNA can't copy itself. Its bases are too tightly bound in their double helix formation to come apart easily. But early on, DNA was able to copy itself by taking advantage of RNA's reactive ability. This happens because DNA and RNA are generally made of the same stuff.

Let's say an RNA strand contains enough energy to collide into a DNA strand and break the bond between the bases that make up the rungs of the DNA ladder. When that happens, the whole DNA string will unravel right down the middle. Now you have two half-strands of DNA that are highly reactive. They immediately attract their complementary bases, and what do you have? Two identical DNA strands, nice and stable again. An original and a copy. This process is even more direct than the several steps RNA needs to copy itself.

RNA strands work like computer programs. The first molecule in line starts a reaction, the middle molecules perform whatever function they can, build different proteins, for example, and the last molecule stops the reaction. Because RNA can only react with its complements, the results are always the same. Because RNA and DNA are so similar, RNA can bump into DNA and get DNA to act like a computer program too.

Over time, those cells where DNA controlled when and how RNA was to behave in the cell survived better than the cells where RNA was less controlled and reactive. Scientists calculate that RNA makes about one mistake per every ten thousand nucleotides copied. DNA using RNA makes only one error per one hundred thousand copies. Given billions of years and the pressure to survive, this tiny difference enabled DNA to become the ruler of the world. Sorry, RNA.

Appendix 2

The Ideasphere: A Practical Application

Social Media

Translating our current ideasphere into an idealsphere is a little more complicated than just adding an L. I've developed a simple process for how to think about issues and develop solutions that maximize choice and minimize harm. Here is my brief reference guide:

First, I make sure the primary goal is firmly established in my mind:

People ought to be free to create any idea and convert it to any action they choose, as long as their actions do not harm other people or the society as a whole.

Now, the thought process:
1. Remember the primary goal
2. Define the current problem in the ideasphere
3. Determine how the ecosystem would address the issue
4. Redefine the ideasphere goal in terms of the issue
5. Outline strategies for using competition, collaboration, and coordination to achieve the goal

6. For coordination changes, add rules and enforcement actions that might be needed
7. Add any additional thoughts about the issue you might want to address

To test out the model, I decided to focus on one problem we have in society today. There are so many to choose from, but I selected social media as my test subject. So, here are the seven steps in action:

Social Media
1. <u>The primary goal:</u> People can implement any idea as long as their actions do not harm others or society.
2. <u>The issue:</u> Some posts may be harmful while others are benign, and they are all mixed together.
3. <u>Ecosystem solution</u>: All "posts" made by cells are sent to the neural system. The neural system determines the potential for harm and responds to the harmful behavior by disallowing it or mitigating its spread. The neural system allows nonharmful posts without constraint.
4. <u>Redefine the goal:</u> People should be free to post whatever they want on social media as long as the post does not harm others or the society.
5. <u>Solution using the three Cs</u>: The social media companies operate in a competitive environment, but the competitive environment does not prevent harmful posts from existing. In social media, the customers are the advertisers who pay the social media company to be on the platform to promote their products. The social

media company's products are the people who post messages, or more precisely, their posts that carry ads. Neither the advertising customers nor the social media company care about the posts people make; they only care about how many people see the ads. So, the more viral a post is, the better, regardless of the nature of the post. The problem is the post itself may be benign or harmful. Coordination is required to prevent harmful actions that may emerge from this arrangement.

6. Rules and Enforcement: The key here is to understand what "speech" is. Speech is an action. It is one way an idea can be implemented. If the speech is merely spoken out into the world, it is not stored anywhere outside the body. But if speech is written or recorded, as in a social media post, it becomes a tangible, physical object that has an existence of its own. That tangible, physical product can be stored and shared by many people. It can influence others. It can benefit others. Think of a new cure for a disease or a study on how bees benefit agriculture. But that tangible, physical product can also harm others. Think of online bullying of a child or fomenting armed rebellion against the government. Online posts run the gamut between the two extremes of benefit and harm. On the one hand, a person can share a picture of a cute puppy. On the other hand, a person can promote a bleach cocktail to treat COVID-19. One of these two is harmful, and I'm pretty sure it's not the adorable puppy gif. It's important to distinguish between freedom of

thought and freedom of speech. Freedom of thought should always be 100% free. People should have the unrestricted freedom to think whatever ideas they want to think. This is our nature. This is our superpower. It should be unfettered and protected. But when speech is turned into physical form, whether it's a social media post, a newspaper, a talk show, or a podcast, it crosses into a new territory where it is an action that can have an existence of its own. This action may be harmless, but it can just as easily be harmful. This shift from an intangible to a tangible form that may be harmful must be addressed, especially as technology continues to change and influence the way we live.

7. <u>Add additional thoughts:</u> The following is the meat of my argument:

Social media is a new phenomenon that is early in its evolutionary development. It is parallel to a new creature evolving in the ecosystem. Since social media is a new twist on the age-old function of speech, let's examine a brief history of how we communicate with each other.

When people began to communicate, they talked. The impact of their speech depended on how well they could be heard. Literally. People stood on soapboxes in town squares or yakked to each other while warming themselves beside the communal fire. Whichever method was used, the reach was understandably limited. Later, when people printed documents and distributed ideas via writing, this reach expanded. Why? When things are written down, they take on an existence of their own. Pamphlets are passed around. Books are borrowed from the library. People read newspapers.

Soon, societies distinguished between two types of writing—news and "not news." We define journalism as the publication of news. News is defined as new or previously unknown information. To be "news" in journalism, the information is required to be provably true. Anything that is not true is defined as "not news." The "not news" writing is a catchall. It's informally referred to as "all the other crap people write." Ironically, many enjoyable and popular offerings fall into this category: fiction, movies, and books about how life can work better if it works like the ecosystem.

Let's focus on journalism for a minute. Journalists came up with their own rules on how to operate, which is interesting in and of itself. It turns out that, back in the day, no one would give up their hard-earned money to read a newspaper that they couldn't trust to tell the truth. The five basic principles of journalism that have evolved are: truth and accuracy, independence, fairness and impartiality, humanity, and accountability. Operating by these rules is a win-win situation for journalists and readers. Journalists are paid to tell the truth, and readers pay to learn the truth.

It wasn't long before some newspapers discovered they could make decent money dressing up an idea as "truth-like" to persuade people to think a specific way. Swaying people to favor one set of ideas over another wasn't new, but using journalism as a cover was. This change had a significant impact. Newspapers and books, and soon to be joined by radio and television, reached far more people than a soapbox. Untruthful ideas that appeared to be truthful had the potential to harm a lot of people. So, governments stepped in to regulate journalism in the cases where they published stories that might cause harm. For example, if journalists lied about a person and caused financial or reputational harm, libel laws protected those victims.

In 1927, after radio became popular, the federal government created the Fairness Doctrine, which regulated news reported over the airwaves. This law required broadcasters to cover controversial issues of public importance and to give fair coverage to opposing views of these issues. The goal of this law was to create an informed society. Lawmakers wanted to make sure citizens received a full and fair view of important issues. Congress abolished this law in 1987. Cable television had made the law moot, anyway. Cable TV does not go over the airwaves, so cable companies were not required to comply with the law.

When it was in effect, the Fairness Doctrine forced broadcasters to be honest in their coverage. After the law was abolished, media companies were free to return to the much murkier world of putting out "news" that was neither true nor independent nor fair nor human nor accountable. In other words, they produced "not-journalism" dressed up as journalism.

Social media is the next generation of information producers, and it's a doozy. It mixes all types of information into one big pot, and it mixes people who post information into another big pot. Let's take a closer look at this strange amalgamation of communication.

Who can post on social media? Anyone. What can they post? Pretty much anything. I can post a picture of my dog on my account and tell the world how cute he is. On my very same account, I can also post my opinion that our recent election was corrupt, and the government should be overthrown. And I can post anything in between. Some posts are harmless. Some are harmful. Others are somewhere in the middle.

So, here's where we stand right now. We have a forum in which a person can act as a journalist, and that very same person can act as a producer of "all the other crap people write." It's all mixed up in a giant messy blob of posts streaming out of millions of social media accounts every minute of every day.

How would the ecosystem handle this? Well, first, cells can only communicate with other cells when it's useful to the survival of the other cells or the body as a whole. If we took this tactic, we could wipe out 99.9% of all social media posts because they are mostly useless crap. But given that people are people, and they should be allowed to share useless crap if they want to, this option is out. Cells don't do useless. But people? We're really good at useless.

So, the job of sorting out the mess that is social media is left to our coordinating function. Yup, it's another area where government should regulate. But there's a catch. Some of the content on social media is harmless, and therefore the right to post should be maximized. Some of it, however, is harmful and should be subject to regulation. So, the answer is easy-peasy—just separate the harmless from the harmful and regulate the harmful. Sure, there are only twelve gazillion posts coming out every minute. No problem!

So, let's try this; let's do it the ecosystem way. We make the cells, I mean, people, report on the truthfulness of their posts. The government makes a simple set of rules and requires the social media companies to enforce those rules.

Rule #1: Every person who posts must describe their post as either:
- true, that is, based on evidence that has been proven, OR
- not true; that is, it is not proven or is the opinion of the posting person

Rule #2: Every person must take responsibility for their post.

After a person writes a post but before sending it out into the social media world, a pop-up window prompts the person to provide additional information about the post.

Let's consider some examples.

Post:	My classmate Bobby Jones is fat and ugly
I must also state:	This is not a true statement. This is my opinion. I take responsibility for posting this untruthful message.

You might as well post "I'm a jerk." But I digress. The point is that the person who posts is required to describe the truthfulness of the post and their accountability for posting it. The speech itself is not prohibited. The required disclosure, however, makes it clear that the person who posts it is accountable for the content of the statement.

Let's take another example. Let's say I share a post from someone who already identified their post as a non-true opinion:

Post:	A certain politician is a pedophile.
I must also state:	This is not a true statement. This is my opinion. I take responsibility for posting this untruthful message.

In this case, you might want to post, "I'm a super jerk." The point is, free speech is not infringed, but the untruthfulness and responsibility of the post are noted.

Now, for a true post:

Post:	This dog in Seattle rode the bus to the dog park by himself
I must also state:	This is a true statement; I have accurately stated the facts.
	I take responsibility for posting this truthful message

Now, you may argue that people who are unable to distinguish between truth and lie will not describe their posts honestly. I agree with you. So, our regulators need to anticipate this and put some teeth into enforcement.

Enforcement Rule #1: People who respond to a post may dispute an inaccurate description and report their dispute to the social media company.

Enforcement Rule #2: If a person posts a false description, they receive a warning from the social media company.

Enforcement Rule #3: Those who inaccurately describe or comment receive a warning from the social media company. Those who inaccurately dispute a description or comment are warned as well.

Enforcement Rule #4: If the "inaccurate poster" or an "inaccurate disputer" repeatedly posts false comments, they are removed from the social media platform.

Let me anticipate the screams of indignation. Free Speech! I can hear it now. You are violating a person's right to free speech. And I would respond, absolutely not. People are still free to speak, but the speech is now infused with accountability. You can still speak, but now you are required to accurately describe your speech. As a person who posts on social media, you are allowed to speak as both a journalist and an "other crap" person. Therefore, it is up to you to tell the people who read your post in which capacity you're speaking. That's not a violation of your free speech; that's a protection for others from your potentially dangerous, physically existing, free-flowing action you call speech that is actually a tangible social media post with a life of its own. This is a way for people who read your posts to distinguish whether your post is truthful or just a bunch of crap. You, the person who posts, knows this best, so it is your job to say.

Then there's the "What is truth, really?" argument. Without going all existential on you, journalists deal with this problem every day. Journalists must prove that what they say is true. If they're wrong, they are required to run a retraction. Now, here's where you argue that you're not a journalist, you're just a simple citizen making a post. To which I would respond that if you are going to act like a journalist, you need to follow the rules of a journalist. If you are not going to act like a journalist, call your post an opinion and move on. What you shouldn't be allowed to do is act like a journalist without the rigor of a journalist. Sorry, no can do. If you can't prove what you say, you belong in the "other crap" department, I mean the opinion department.

The last argument, promoted by the social media companies themselves, is: "This is too hard." Nope. If you can set up a vehicle

The Ideasphere: A Practical Application

by which people can post, you can set up a vehicle by which people can describe their posts. Furthermore, you might need a few disclosure rules yourself. How many people posted harmful content? How many people lied about their posts? How many people got kicked off the platform? How many people should have been kicked off but weren't? How many of those who post are actually people? This kind of information would be useful to all of us who suffer from disinformation.

Hmm, it might be useful if some news organizations on radio and television or politicians or CEOs were required to describe published content in this way too. Any speech that is reproduced in a physical form should be subject to this rule. Hmm. I'd like to hear Donald Trump post on his social media platform, "The election was rigged. This is my opinion and not a proven fact. Also, I am aware I'm just making this shit up." That might be refreshing.

Sources

Introduction

1. Louis A. Warren, ed., "Lincoln's Manual for Executives," *Lincoln Lore*, no. 289, October 22, 1934, https://www.friendsofthelincolncollection.org/wp-content/uploads/2018/07/LL_1934-10-22_01.pdf.

2. Jessica Harwood and Douglas Wilkin, "4.12 Geologic Time Scale," *flexbooks.ck-12*, June 1, 2020, https://flexbooks.ck12.org/cbook/ck-12-middle-school-life-science-2.0/section/4.12/primary/lesson/timeline-of-evolution-ms-ls/.

3. Duke University, "Tree Of Life' For 2.3 Million Species Released," *Phys.Org*, September 19, 2015, https://phys.org/news/2015-09-tree-life-million-species.html

4. World Health Organization, "The Latest State Of Food Security And Nutrition Report Shows The World Is Moving Backwards In Efforts To Eliminate Hunger And Malnutrition,"

World Health Organization, July 6, 2022, https://www.who.int/news/item/06-07-2022-un-report--global-hunger-numbers-rose-to-as-many-as-828-million-in-2021#:~:text=As%20many%20as%20828%20million%20people%20were%20-affected%20by%20hunger,9.8%25%20of%20the%20world%20population

5. "The Effects of Climate Change," *NASA*, accessed October 22, 2022, https://climate.nasa.gov/effects/.

6. Amy Watson, "False News In The U.S. - Statistics & Facts," *Statista.com*, January 9,2024, https://www.statista.com/topics/3251/fake-news/#topicOverview

7. Chad Stone, Danilo Trisi, Arloc Sherman, and Jennifer Beltrán, "A Guide to Statistics on Historical Trends in Income Inequality," *Center on Budget and Policy Priorities*, updated January 13, 2020, https://www.cbpp.org/research/poverty-and-inequality/a-guide-to-statistics-on-historical-trends-in-income-inequality

8. Michael Rothschild, *Bionomics: Economy As Ecosystem* (New York: Henry Holt, 1990), xi-xv, 1-12.

Chapter 1

1. U.S. Energy Information, Administration, "What Is Energy?" *U.S. Energy Information, Administration*, August 16, 2023, https://www.eia.gov/energyexplained/what-is-energy/

2. Larry M. Silverberg, "Physicists Suggest All Matter May Be Made Up of Energy 'Fragments,'" *Science Alert*, December 11, 2020, https://www.sciencealert.com/physicists-suggest-energy-fragments-is-the-best-way-to-describe-matter.

3. James Trefil, *1001 Things Everyone Should Know About Science* (New York: Doubleday, 1992), 265.

4. Yoshinari Hayato and Yumiko Takenaga, "Were All Forces, Electromagnetic Force and Gravity, Originally One?" Kamioka Observatory, ICRR, The University of Tokyo, accessed December 20, 2023, https://www-sk.icrr.u-tokyo.ac.jp/en/hk/special/yonde04/.

5. Joseph McClain, "The Weak Force: Life Couldn't Exist Without It," *William and Mary*, November 14, 2018, https://www.wm.edu/news/stories/2018/the-weak-force-life-couldnt-exist-without-it.php#:~:text=He%20pointed%20out%20that%20the,drives%20the%20sun's%20nuclear%20furnace.

6. U.S. Energy Information, Administration, "Electricity Explained," *U.S. Energy Information, Administration*, December 19, 2022, https://www.eia.gov/energyexplained/

electricity/the-science-of-electricity.php#:~:text=Electrons%20are%20held%20in%20their,both%20carry%20an%20electrical%20charge.

7. Swinburne University of Technology, "Laws of Physics Vary Throughout the Universe, New Study Suggests," *ScienceDaily*, September 9, 2010, www.sciencedaily.com/releases/2010/09/100909004112.htm.

8. CERN, "The Standard Model," Exploratorium, September 16, 2022, https://www.exploratorium.edu/origins/cern/ideas/standard3.html.

9. Science Programming On Air and Online, "E=mc^2 Explained," *NOVA*, August 2005, https://www.pbs.org/wgbh/nova/einstein/lrk-hand-emc2expl.html.

10. Trefil, *1001 Things Everyone Should Know About Science*, 249–55.

11. David Roeder, "What Are Pool Balls Made Of?" Blatt Billiards, September 29, 2021, https://blattbilliards.com/blogs/news/what-are-pool-balls-made-of.

12. "The Universe's History," *NASA Science Universe Exploration*, acces2sed December 20, 2023, https://universe.nasa.gov/universe/basics/.

13. Michael D. Lemonick, "How Analyzing Cosmic Nothing Might Explain Everything," *SciAm* January 1, 2024, https://www.scientificamerican.com/article/how-analyzing-cosmic-nothing-might-explain-everything/

14. Iqbal Pittalwala, "Scientists Precisely Measure Total Amount of Matter in the Universe," *Phys*, September 28, 2020, https://phys.org/news/2020-09-scientists-precisely-total-amount-universe.html.

15. Robert Lea, "What Is Dark Energy?" *Space.com*, November 24, 2022, https://www.space.com/dark-energy-what-is-it

16. Paul Scott Anderson, "A New Look at the Universe's Oldest Light," *EarthSky*, January 12, 2021, https://earthsky.org/space/a-new-look-at-the-universes-oldest-light/.

17. Trefil, *1001 Things Everyone Should Know About Science*, 252.

18. Charles Q Choi, "How Did Multicellular Life Evolve?" *Astrobiology at NASA*, February 13, 2017, https://astrobiology.nasa.gov/news/how-did-multicellular-life-evolve/#:~:text="Unicellularity%20is%20clearly%20successful%20—%20unicellular,Fe%20Institute%20in%20New%20Mexico.

19. Ken Stewart, "Laws of Thermodynamics," Britannica, May 27, 2024, https://www.britannica.com/science/laws-of-thermodynamics.

20. Stephen Jay Gould, *Wonderful Life: The Burgess Shale and the Nature of History* (New York: W. W. Norton & Company, 1989), 289–91.

Chapter 2

1. "The Earliest Atmosphere," *Smithsonian Environmental Research Center*, accessed September 17, 2022, https://forces.si.edu/atmosphere/02_02_01.html.

2. John Wenz, "Scientists Find Strong Evidence That the Earth Was Hit Head-On by a Mars-Sized Planet," *Popular Mechanics*, January 28, 2016, https://www.popularmechanics.com/space/a19143/earth-moon-theia-collision/.

3. Richard Meckien, "When a Day Lasted Only 4 Hours," Institute of Advanced Studies of the University of Sao Paulo, March 16, 2016, http://www.iea.usp.br/en/news/when-a-day-lasted-only-four-hours.

4. Jessica Stoller-Conrad, "How Far Away Is the Moon?" *NASA Science Space Place*, accessed September 20, 2022, https://spaceplace.nasa.gov/moon-distance/en/.

5. Marina Koren, "The Moon Is Leaving Us," *The Atlantic*, September 30, 2021, https://www.theatlantic.com/science/archive/2021/09/moon-moving-away-earth/620254/.

6. Alfredo Carpineti, "Fragments of the Planet That Formed the Moon May Be Buried by the Earth's Core," *IFL Science*, March 26, 2021, https://www.iflscience.com/fragments-of-the-planet-that-formed-the-moon-may-be-buried-by-the-earths-core-59172.

7. John Baez, "The Earth—for Physicists," *Physics World*, August 2009, https://math.ucr.edu/home/baez/physics_world_earth.pdf.

8. Alan Buis, "Earth's Magnetosphere: Protecting Our Planet from Harmful Space Energy," *NASA Jet Propulsion Laboratory*, August 3, 2021, https://climate.nasa.gov/news/3105/earths-magnetosphere-protecting-our-planet-from-harmful-space-energy/.

9. "Early Earth's Atmosphere and Oceans," *Lunar Planetary Institute*, accessed August 17, 2024, https://www.lpi.usra.edu/education/timeline/gallery/slide_17.html

10. Hannah Hickey, "Volcanic Eruptions May Have Spurred First 'Whiffs' of Oxygen in Earth's Atmosphere," *UW News*, August 25, 2021, https://www.washington.edu/news/2021/08/25/volcanic-eruptions-may-have-spurred-first-whiffs-of-oxygen-in-earths-atmosphere/.

11. Catherine Brahic, "Volcanic Mayhem Drove Major Burst of Evolution," *New Scientist,* January 15, 2014, https://www.newscientist.com/article/mg22129522-600-volcanic-mayhem-drove-major-burst-of-evolution/.

Chapter 3

1. Norio Kitadai and Shigenori Maruyama, "Origins of Building Blocks of Life: A Review," *Geoscience Frontiers* 9, no. 4 (2018): 1117–53, https://www.sciencedirect.com/science/article/pii/S1674987117301305.

2. Paul Webb, "Chapter 5.2: Origin of the Oceans," *Introduction to Oceanography* (Pressbooks.pub, 2021), https://rwu.pressbooks.pub/webboceanography/chapter/5-2-origin-of-the-oceans/.

3. Evrim Yazgin, "Scientists Narrow Down the Theory about the Origins of Life—Volcanoes or Meteors," *Cosmos*, May 26, 2023, https://cosmosmagazine.com/earth/meteor-volcano-origin-life/.

4. Joseph A. Resing and Francis J. Sansone, "The Chemistry of Lava–Seawater Interactions: The Generation of Acidity," *Geochimica et Cosmochimica Acta* 63, no. 15 (1999): 2183–98, http://www.soest.hawaii.edu/oceanography/faculty/sansone/Resing & Sansone 1999 GCA.pdf.

5. Jason P. Schrum, Ting F. Zhu, and Jack W. Szostak, "The Origins of Cellular Life," *Cold Spring Harbor Perspectives in Biology 2, no. 9 (2010): a002212, doi:10.1101/cshperspect.a002212*, https://www.ncbi.nlm.nih.gov/pmc/articles/PMC2926753/.

6. Jennifer Newton, "Carbohydrates Promoted in New Prebiotic Theory," *Chemistry World*, September 11, 2017, https://www.chemistryworld.com/news/carbohydrates-promoted-in-new-prebiotic-theory/3007970.article.

7. Michael K. Reddy, "Amino Acid—Chemical Compound," Britannica, August 22, 2022, https://www.britannica.com/science/amino-acid.

8. "The Nutrition Source—Protein," *Harvard T. H. Chan School of Public Health*, accessed September 23, 2022, https://www.hsph.harvard.edu/nutritionsource/what-should-you-eat/protein/.

9. Ana Gutiérrez-Preciado, Hector Romero, and Mariana Peimbert, "An Evolutionary Perspective on Amino Acids," *Nature Education* 3, no. 9 (2010): 29, https://www.nature.com/scitable/topicpage/an-evolutionary-perspective-on-amino-acids-14568445/.

10. Uma Shanker, Brij Bhushan, G. Bhattacharjee, and Kamaluddin, "Formation of Nucleobases from Formamide in the Presence of Iron Oxides: Implication in Chemical Evolution and Origin of Life," *Astrobiology*, April 19, 2011, https://www.liebertpub.com/doi/abs/10.1089/ast.2010.0530.

11. Irene A. Chen and Peter Walde, "From Self-Assembled Vesicles to Protocells," *Cold Spring Harbor Perspectives in Biology* 2, no. 7 (2010): a002170, doi:10.1101/cshperspect.a002170, https://www.ncbi.nlm.nih.gov/pmc/articles/PMC2890201/.

12. Annabelle Biscans, "Exploring the Emergence of RNA Nucleosides and Nucleotides on the Early Earth," *Life (Basel)* 8, no. 4 (2018): 57, doi:10.3390/life8040057, https://www.ncbi.nlm.nih.gov/pmc/articles/PMC6316623/.

13. James Trefil, *1001 Things Everyone Should Know About Science* (New York: Doubleday, 1992), 80.

14. Ying-Wei Yang et al., "Experimental Evidence That GNA and TNA Were Not Sequential Polymers in the Prebiotic Evolution of RNA," *Journal of Molecular Evolution* 65, no. 3 (2007): 289–95, https://pubmed.ncbi.nlm.nih.gov/17828568/.

15. David Wang and Aisha Farhana, "Biochemistry, RNA Structure," in *StatPearls* (Treasure Island, FL: StatPearls Publishing, 2022), https://www.ncbi.nlm.nih.gov/books/NBK558999/.

16. Ruairi J. Mackenzie, "DNA vs. RNA—5 Key Differences and Comparison," *Technology Networks—Genomic Research*, updated January 22, 2024, https://www.technologynetworks.com/genomics/lists/what-are-the-key-differences-between-dna-and-rna-296719.

17. Bruce Alberts et al., "The RNA World and the Origins of Life," in *Molecular Biology of the Cell, 4th ed.* (New York: Garland Science, 2002), https://www.ncbi.nlm.nih.gov/books/NBK26876/.

18. Bruce Alberts et al., "From DNA to RNA," in *Molecular Biology of the Cell*, 4th ed. (New York: Garland Science, 2002), https://www.ncbi.nlm.nih.gov/books/NBK26887/.

Chapter 4

1. Reginald Davey, "What Is a Protocell?" *AZO Life Sciences*, accessed September 23, 2022, https://www.azolifesciences.com/article/What-is-a-Protocell.aspx.

2. Jessica Harwood and Douglas Wilkin, "4.12 Geologic Time Scale," *flexbooks.ck-12*, June 1, 2020, https://flexbooks.ck12.org/cbook/ck-12-middle-school-life-science-2.0/section/4.12/primary/lesson/timeline-of-evolution-ms-ls/.

3. Google Classroom, "Prokaryote Structure," Khan Academy, accessed September 28, 2022, https://www.khanacademy.org/science/ap-biology/gene-expression-and-regulation/dna-and-rna-structure/a/prokaryote-structure.

4. Nicole Gleichmann, "Prokaryotes vs. Eukaryotes: What Are the Key Differences?" *Technology Networks—Cell Science*, July 8, 2021, https://www.technologynetworks.com/cell-science/articles/prokaryotes-vs-eukaryotes-what-are-the-key-differences-336095.

5. Geoffrey M. Cooper, "The Origin and Evolution of Cells," in *The Cell: A Molecular Approach*, 2nd ed. (Sunderland (MA): Sinauer Associates, 2000), https://www.ncbi.nlm.nih.gov/books/NBK9841/.

6. Bruce Alberts et al., "From DNA to RNA," in *Molecular Biology of the Cell, 4th ed.* (New York: Garland Science, 2002), https://www.ncbi.nlm.nih.gov/books/NBK26887/#.

7. Ker Than, "All Species Evolved from Single Cell, Study Finds," *National Geographic*, May 14, 2010, https://www.nationalgeographic.com/adventure/article/100513-science-evolution-darwin-single-ancestor.

8. Wei Liu et al., "From *Saccharomyces cerevisiae* to Human: The Important Gene Co-expression Modules," *Biomedical Report* 7, no. 2 (2017):153–8, https://www.ncbi.nlm.nih.gov/pmc/articles/PMC5525645/Yeast possesseshomologous genes,gene function studies.

9. Elizabeth Burke, "Why Use Zebrafish to Study Human Diseases?" *I Am Intramural Blog*, August 9, 2016, https://irp.nih.gov/blog/post/2016/08/why-use-zebrafish-to-study-human-diseases.

10. "DNA: Comparing Humans and Chimps," American Museum of Natural History, accessed June 27, 2024, https://www.amnh.org/exhibitions/permanent/human-origins/understanding-our-past/dna-comparing-humans-and-chimps.

11. Charles Darwin, *From So Simple a Beginning: Darwin's Four Great Books,* ed. Edward O. Wilson (New York: W. W. Norton and Company, 2006), 488–533.

12. Leslie A. Pray, "DNA Replication and Causes of Mutation," *Nature Education* 1, no. 1 (2008): 214, https://www.nature.com/scitable/topicpage/dna-replication-and-causes-of-mutation.

13. Michael L. McKinney, "How Do Rare Species Avoid Extinction? A Paleontological View," in *The Biology of Rarity*, eds. W. E. Kunin and K. J. Gaston (New York: Chapman & Hall, 1997), 110, accessed June 26, 2024, https://books.google.com/books?id=4LHnCAAAQBAJ&pg=PA110#v=onepage.

14. Joanna Thompson, "How Many Animals Have Ever Existed on Earth?" *LiveScience*, October 8, 2023, https://www.livescience.com/animals/how-many-animals-have-ever-existed-on-earth.

15. Hannah Ritchie, "How Many Species Are There?" *Our World In Data*, November 30, 2022, https://ourworldindata.org/how-many-species-are-there#:~:text=Some%20more%20recent%20studies%20estimate,million%20species%20on%20Earth%20today.

16. David Jablonski, "Extinction: Past and Present," *Nature*, February 12, 2004, https://www.nature.com/articles/427589a.

17. Carl Zimmer, "How Many Cells Are in Your Body?" *National Geographic*, October 23, 2013, https://www.nationalgeographic.com/science/article/how-many-cells-are-in-your-body.

18. Luis Villazon, "When We Die, Does Our Whole Body Die at the Same Time?" *BBC Science Focus*, accessed October 1, 2022, https://www.sciencefocus.com/the-human-body/when-we-die-does-our-whole-body-die-at-the-same-time/.

19. Nabeeha Khalid and Mahzad Azimpouran, *Necrosis* (Treasure Island, FL: StatPearls Publishing, 2022), updated March 6, 2023, https://www.ncbi.nlm.nih.gov/books/NBK557627/.

20. Bruce Alberts et al., "Programmed Cell Death (Apoptosis)" in *Molecular Biology of the Cell, 4th ed.* (New York: Garland Science, 2002), https://www.ncbi.nlm.nih.gov/books/NBK26873/.

21. Rosa Ana Risques and Daniel E. L. Promislow, "All's Well That Ends Well: Why Large Species Have Short Telomeres," *Royal Society Publishing*, January 15, 2018, https://royalsocietypublishing.org/doi/10.1098/rstb.2016.0448.

22. Michael Gardner et al., "Gender and Telomere Length: Systematic Review and Meta-analysis," *Experimental Gerontology* 51 (2014): 15–27, https://www.ncbi.nlm.nih.gov/pmc/articles/PMC4523138/

23. Jason P. Schrum, Ting F. Zhu, and Jack W. Szostak, "The Origins of Cellular Life," *Cold Spring Harbor Perspectives in Biology* 2, no. 9 (2010): a002212, *doi:10.1101/cshperspect.a002212,* https://www.ncbi.nlm.nih.gov/pmc/articles/PMC2926753/.

24. Michael Pollen, *Food Rules: An Eater's Manual* (New York: Penguin Books, 2009).

25. Gavin Van De Walle, "9 Important Functions of Protein in Your Body," *HealthLine*, updated February 15, 2023, https://www.healthline.com/nutrition/functions-of-protein.

26. "The Nutrition Source—Carbohydrates," *Harvard T. H. Chan School of Public Health*, accessed September 23, 2022, https://www.hsph.harvard.edu/nutritionsource/carbohydrates/.

27. Anne Helmenstine, "What Is the Most Abundant Element in the Universe?" *Science Notes*, October 27, 2020, https://sciencenotes.org/what-is-the-most-abundant-element-in-the-universe/.

28. Oxford University Museum of Natural History, "Bacterial World," *University of Oxford*, October 19, 2018, http://www.oum.ox.ac.uk/bacterialworld/.

29. Hannah Ritchie, "Humans Make Up Just 0.01% of Earth's Life—What's the Rest?" *Our World in Data*, April 24, 2019, https://ourworldindata.org/life-on-earth.

30. Bill Chappell, "Along with Humans, Who Else Is in the 7 Billion Club?" *The Two-Way, NPR*, November 3, 2011, https://www.npr.org/sections/thetwo-way/2011/11/03/141946751/along-with-humans-who-else-is-in-the-7-billion-club.

31. Bert Markgraf, "The Major Structural Advantage Eukaryotes Have Over Prokaryotes," *Sciencing*, July 31, 2019, https://sciencing.com/major-structural-advantage-eukaryotes-over-prokaryotes-14989.html.

32. Charles Q. Choi, "How Did Multicellular Life Evolve?" *Astrobiology at NASA*, February 13, 2017, https://astrobiology.nasa.gov/news/how-did-multicellular-life-evolve/.

33. Jamie Ellis, "The Internal Anatomy of the Honey Bee," *American Bee Journal*, September 1, 2015, https://americanbeejournal.com/the-internal-anatomy-of-the-honey-bee/.

34. Darwin, *From So Simple a Beginning*, 489–502.

35. Michael Rothschild, *Bionomics: The Inevitability of Capitalism* (New York: Henry Holt, 1990), 40, 62, 207.

Chapter 5

1. National Geographic Education, "Ecosystem," *National Geographic*, accessed June 28, 2024, https://education.nationalgeographic.org/resource/ecosystem/.

2. Charles Darwin, *From So Simple a Beginning: Darwin's Four Great Books,* ed. Edward O. Wilson (New York: W. W. Norton and Company, 2006), 488–500.

3. Michael Rothschild, *Bionomics: The Inevitability of Capitalism* (New York: Henry Holt, 1990), 205–12.

4. Darwin, *From So Simple a Beginning*, 501–33.

5. Darwin, *From So Simple a Beginning*, 324–47.

6. "History of Galápagos," *Galápagos Conservancy*, accessed October 6, 2022, https://www.galapagos.org/about_galapagos/history/.

7. Rothschild, *Bionomics*, 54–63.

8. Pattie Thomas, "Working the Night Shift—Bats Play an Important Role in Pollinating Crops," *US Department of Agriculture*, October 29, 2014, https://www.usda.gov/media/blog/2014/10/29/working-night-shift-bats-play-important-role-pollinating-crops.

9. Erika Engelhaupt, "How Human Violence Stacks Up Against Other Killer Animals," *National Geographic*, September 28, 2016, https://www.nationalgeographic.com/science/article/human-violence-evolution-animals-nature-science.

10. Rachel M. McCoy, Joshua R. Widhal, Gordon G. McNickle,"Allelopathy As An Evolutionary Game," *Plant Direct*, February 11, 2022, https://www.ncbi.nlm.nih.gov/pmc/articles/PMC8832168/

Chapter 6

1. Jason P. Schrum, Ting F. Zhu, and Jack W. Szostak, "The Origins of Cellular Life," *Cold Spring Harbor Perspectives in Biology 2, no. 9 (2010): a002212, doi:10.1101/cshperspect. a002212* https://www.ncbi.nlm.nih.gov/pmc/articles/PMC2926753/.

2. Bruce Alberts et al., "Fractionation of Cells," in *Molecular Biology of the Cell, 4th ed.* (New York: Garland Science, 2002), https://www.ncbi.nlm.nih.gov/books/NBK26936/.

3. G. M. Cooper, "The Origin and Evolution of Cells," *The Cell: A Molecular Approach, 2nd ed.* (Sunderland, MA: Sinauer Associates, 2000), https://www.ncbi.nlm.nih.gov/books/NBK9841/.

4. John Staughton, "How Long Did It Take for Multicellular Life to Evolve from Unicellular Life?" *Science ABC*, last updated October 19, 2023, https://www.scienceabc.com/pure-sciences/how-long-did-it-take-for-multicellular-life-to-evolve-from-unicellular-life.html.

5. Bert Markgraf, "The Major Structural Advantage Eukaryotes Have Over Prokaryotes," *Sciencing*, July 31, 2019, https://sciencing.com/major-structural-advantage-eukaryotes-over-prokaryotes-14989.html.

6. Google Classroom, "Prokaryote Metabolism," Khan Academy, accessed September 28, 2022, https://www.khanacademy.org/science/biology/bacteria-archaea/prokaryote-metabolism-ecology/a/prokaryote-metabolism-nutrition.

7. William B. Whitman, David C. Coleman, and William J. Wiebe, "Prokaryotes: The Unseen Majority," *Proceedings of the National Academy of Sciences USA* 95, no. 12 (1998): 6578–83, doi: 10.1073/pnas.95.12.6578, https://www.ncbi.nlm.nih.gov/pmc/articles/PMC33863/.

8. Jordi van Gestel, Martin A. Nowak, and Corina E. Tarnita, "The Evolution of Cell-to-Cell Communication in a Sporulating Bacterium," *PLOS Computational Biology* 8, no. 12 (2012): e1002818, https://journals.plos.org/ploscompbiol/article?id=10.1371/journal.pcbi.1002818.

9. "Dictionary: Sexual Reproduction," *Biology Online*, accessed October 9, 2022, https://www.biologyonline.com/dictionary/sexual-reproduction.

10. Carlos J. Melián et al., "Does Sex Speed Up Evolutionary Rate and Increase Biodiversity?" *PLOS Computational Biology 8, no. 3 (2012): e1002414,* https://www.ncbi.nlm.nih.gov/pmc/articles/PMC3297559/.

11. "The Evolution of Early Animal Complexity," George Washington University, accessed October 9, 2022, https://www2.gwu.edu/~darwin/BiSc151/NoCoelom/earlyanimal.html.

12. Carl Zimmer, "To Bee," Carl Zimmer, October 25, 2006, https://carlzimmer.com/to-bee/.

13. Jamie Ellis, "The Internal Anatomy of the Honey Bee," *American Bee Journal*, September 1, 2015, https://americanbeejournal.com/the-internal-anatomy-of-the-honey-bee/.

14. Marcelo Gleiser, "The Microbial Eve: Our Oldest Ancestors Were Single-Celled Organisms," *NPR*, January 31, 2018, https://www.npr.org/sections/13.7/2018/01/31/581874421/be-humbled-our-oldest-ancestors-were-single-celled-organisms.

15. Bernd Heinrich, *Bumblebee Economics* (Cambridge, MA: Harvard University Press, 1979, 2004), 7–37.

16. Michael Rothschild, *Bionomics: The Inevitability of Capitalism* (New York: Henry Holt, 1990), 91–98.

17. Yinon M. Bar-On, Rob Phillips, and Ron Milo, "The Biomass Distribution on Earth," *Proceedings of the National Academy of Sciences* 115, no. 25 (2018): 6506–6511, https://www.ncbi.nlm.nih.gov/pmc/articles/PMC6016768/.

18. Bill Chappell, "Along With Humans, Who Else Is in the 7 Billion Club?" *The Two-Way, NPR*, November 3, 2011, https://www.npr.org/sections/thetwo-way/2011/11/03/141946751/along-with-humans-who-else-is-in-the-7-billion-club.

19. "Cell Biology by the Numbers—How Many Cells Are There in an Organism?" Bionumbers, accessed October 10, 2022, http://book.bionumbers.org/how-many-cells-are-there-in-an-organism/.

Chapter 7

1. Michael Rothschild, *Bionomics: The Inevitability of Capitalism* (New York: Henry Holt, 1990), 91–98.

2. A. O. Spakov, M. N. Pertseva, "Signal Transduction Systems of Prokaryotes," *Zhurnal Évolyutsionnoy Biokhimii i Fiziologii* 44, no. 2 (2008): 113–30, PMID: 18669273, https://pubmed.ncbi.nlm.nih.gov/18669273/.

3. Pedro C. Marijuán, Jorge Navarro, and Raquel del Moral B., "How Prokaryotes 'Encode' Their Environment: Systemic Tools for Organizing the Information Flow," *ResearchGate*, October 2017, https://www.researchgate.net/publication/320320195_How_prokaryotes_their_environment.

4. Gabe Buckley, "Cell Signaling," *Biology Dictionary*, January 15, 2021, https://biologydictionary.net/cell-signaling/.

5. David Robson, "A Brief History of the Brain," *New Scientist*, September 21, 2011, https://www.newscientist.com/article/mg21128311-800-a-brief-history-of-the-brain/.

6. Charlotte Swanson, "Bizarre Brains of the Animal Kingdom," *Science World*, February 1, 2022, https://www.scienceworld.ca/stories/bizarre-brains-animal-kingdom/.

7. Jon Lieff, "The Remarkable Bee Brain," *JonLieffMD*, November 12, 2012, https://jonlieffmd.com/blog/the-remarkable-bee-brain-2.

8. Jamie Ellis, "The Internal Anatomy of the Honey Bee," *American Bee Journal*, September 1, 2015, https://americanbeejournal.com/the-internal-anatomy-of-the-honey-bee/.

9. "Number of Neurons in the Brain of Animals," *DinoAnimals*, accessed October 12, 2022, https://dinoanimals.com/animals/number-of-neurons-in-the-brain-of-animals/.

10. Bernd Heinrich, *Bumblebee Economics* (Cambridge, MA: Harvard University Press, 1979), 8–16.

11. Rothschild, *Bionomics*, 155–64.

12. "Meninges," *Cleveland Clinic*, January 11, 2022, https://my.clevelandclinic.org/health/articles/22266-meninges.

13. "Cell Signaling: How Your Cells Talk to Each Other," *Ask The Scientists*, accessed October 12, 2022, https://askthescientists.com/qa/what-is-cell-signaling/.

14. Aaron Kandola, "What Is the Autonomic Nervous System?" *Medical News Today*, January 10, 2020, https://www.medicalnewstoday.com/articles/327450.

15. "DNA Responds to Signals from Outside the Cell," *DNA from the Beginning*, accessed October 12, 2022, http://www.dnaftb.org/35/.

16. Kimberly Repp, "How the Body Repairs Itself," *Arizona State University—Ask a Biologist,* accessed October 12, 2022, https://askabiologist.asu.edu/explore/when-body-attacked.

17. Susan Elmore, "Apoptosis: A Review of Programmed Cell Death," *Toxicologic Pathology* 35, no. 4 (2007): 495–516. doi: 10.1080/01926230701320337, https://www.ncbi.nlm.nih.gov/pmc/articles/PMC2117903/.

18. Nabeeha Khalid and Mahzad Azimpouran, "Necrosis," in *StatPearls* [Internet], (Treasure Island, FL: StatPearls Publishing, 2022), updated March 9, 2022, https://www.ncbi.nlm.nih.gov/books/NBK557627/.

19. Editorial Staff, "How Many Possible Moves Are There in Chess?" *Chess Journal*, accessed October 13, 2022, https://www.chessjournal.com/how-many-possible-moves-are-there-in-chess/

20. Rothschild, *Bionomics*, 91–98.

21. Rob DeSalle and Ian Tattersall, "Do Plants Have Brains?" *Natural History*, accessed October 13, 2022, https://www.naturalhistorymag.com/features/152208/do-plants-have-brains.

22. Michael Laub, "Keeping Signals Straight: How Cells Process Information and Make Decisions," *PLOS Biology* 14, no. 7 (2016), https://journals.plos.org/plosbiology/article?id=10.1371/journal.pbio.1002519.

23. "The Information in DNA Is Decoded by Transcription," Nature Education, accessed October 13, 2022, https://www.nature.com/scitable/topicpage/the-information-in-dna-is-decoded-by-6524808/.

Chapter 8

1. "Data vs. Information," Diffen, accessed October 13, 2022, https://www.diffen.com/difference/Data_vs_Information.

2. Gazette Staff, "Why Onions Have More DNA Than You Do," *Harvard Gazette*, February 10, 2000, https://news.harvard.edu/gazette/story/2000/02/why-onions-have-more-dna-than-you-do/.

3. Michael Rothschild, *Bionomics: The Inevitability of Capitalism* (New York: Henry Holt, 1990), 1–12.

4. Rothschild, *Bionomics*, 155–64.

5. Charles Darwin, *From So Simple a Beginning: Darwin's Four Great Books*, ed. Edward O. Wilson (New York: W. W. Norton and Company, 2006), 582–605.

6. James Trefil, *1001 Things Everyone Should Know About Science* (New York: Doubleday, 1992), 15–17.

7. Michael Laub, "Keeping Signals Straight: How Cells Process Information and Make Decisions," *PLOS Biology* 14, no. 7 (2016), https://journals.plos.org/plosbiology/article?id=10.1371/journal.pbio.1002519.

8. "The Information in DNA Is Decoded by Transcription," *Nature Education*, accessed October 13, 2022, https://www.nature.com/scitable/topicpage/the-information-in-dna-is-decoded-by-6524808/.

9. Richard C. Mohs, "How Human Memory Works," *HowStuffWorks*, accessed October 14, 2022, https://science.howstuffworks.com/life/inside-the-mind/human-brain/human-memory.htm.

10. Darwin, *From So Simple a Beginning*, 489–533.

11. Andrea Stephenson, Justin W. Adams, and Mauro Vaccarezza, "The Vertebrate Heart: An Evolutionary Perspective," *Journal of Anatomy* 231, no. 6 (2017): 787–97, https://onlinelibrary.wiley.com/doi/10.1111/joa.12687.

12. Rothschild, *Bionomics*, 258–59.

13. Neil Shubin, *Your Inner Fish: A Journey Into the 3.5-Billion-Year History of the Human Body* (New York: Vintage Books, 2008), 81–96.

14. Mohs, "How Human Memory Works."

15. University of California—San Diego, "They Remember: Communities of Microbes Found to Have Working Memory," *ScienceDaily*, April 28, 2020, https://www.sciencedaily.com/releases/2020/04/200428093506.htm.

16. Rothschild, *Bionomics*, 117–26.

17. Rothschild, *Bionomics*, 91–98.

Chapter 10

1. Dennis O'Neil, "The First Primates," *Behavioral Sciences Department, Palomar College*, 2014, https://www.palomar.edu/anthro/earlyprimates/early_2.htm.

2. "Evolution of Modern Humans," *Your Genome*, accessed July 21, 2021, https://www.yourgenome.org/stories/evolution-of-modern-humans/.

3. Press Association, "Ancestor of Humans and Other Mammals Was Small Furry Insect Eater," *The Guardian*, February 7, 2013, https://www.theguardian.com/science/2013/feb/07/ancestor-humans-mammals-insect-eater.

4. Michael Rothschild, *Bionomics: The Inevitability of Capitalism* (New York: Henry Holt, 1990), 65–71.

5. Rothschild, *Bionomics*, 160–63.

6. Alison George, "Code Hidden in Stone Age Art May Be the Root of Human Writing," *New Scientist*, November 9, 2016, https://www.newscientist.com/article/mg23230990-700-in-search-of-the-very-first-coded-symbols/.

7. Gwen DeWar, "Newborn Cognitive Development: What Are Babies Thinking and Learning?" *Parenting Science*, 2020, https://parentingscience.com/newborn-cognitive-development/.

Chapter 11

1. Traci Watson, "Ancient Egyptian Cemetery Holds Proof of Hard Labor," *National Geographic*, March 14, 2013, https://www.nationalgeographic.com/history/article/130313-ancient-egypt-akhenaten-amarna-cemetery-archaeology-science-world.

2. Jake Buehler, "The Complex Truth About 'Junk DNA,'" *Quanta Magazine*, September 1, 2021, https://www.quantamagazine.org/the-complex-truth-about-junk-dna-20210901/.

3. Charlotte Hsu, "Carnivorous Plant Throws Out 'Junk' DNA," *University at Buffalo*, May 13, 2013, https://www.buffalo.edu/news/releases/2013/05/023.html.

4. Michael Graw, "Why DNA Is the Most Favorable Molecule for Genetic Material & How RNA Compares to It in This Respect," *Sciencing*, March 13, 2018, https://sciencing.com/dna-favorable-molecule-genetic-material-rna-compares-respect-17806.html.

5. Neha Verma, "Why did Greeks Stopped Worshiping Greek Gods?" *Medium*, February 19, 2024, https://musinghiraeth.medium.com/why-did-greeks-stopped-worshiping-greek-gods-1abcb54d127a

Chapter 12

1. Aishwarya Ahuja, "How Are Memories Stored and Retrieved?" *Science ABC*, updated April 16, 2024, https://www.scienceabc.com/humans/how-are-memory-stored-retrieved.html.

2. "Life Expectancy," *WorldData.info*, accessed October 17, 2022, https://www.worlddata.info/life-expectancy.php (Data is based on the year 2020.)

3. Kendra Cherry, "The Story of Genie Wiley," *Very Well Mind*, updated March 13, 2024, https://www.verywellmind.com/genie-the-story-of-the-wild-child-2795241.

Chapter 13

1. History.com editors, "Social Darwinism," *History*, August 21, 2018, https://www.history.com/topics/early-20th-century-us/social-darwinism.

2. Catherine Wilson, "Darwinian Morality," *Evolution: Education and Outreach*, August 7, 2009, https://evolution-outreach.biomedcentral.com/articles/10.1007/s12052-009-0162-z.

3. "How Do We Know That Humans Are the Major Cause of Global Warming?" *Union of Concerned Scientists*, January 21, 2021, https://www.ucsusa.org/resources/are-humans-major-cause-global-warming.

4. Max Roser, Joe Hasell, Bastian Herre, and Bobbie Macdonald, "War and Peace," *OurWorldInData*, 2024, https://ourworldindata.org/war-and-peace#citation.

5. Ryan Patrick Hanley, "On Self Interest," *Princeton University Press*, June 30, 2021, https://press.princeton.edu/ideas/on-self-interest.

Chapters 14 and 15

1. Mark Buchanan, "Wealth Happens," *Harvard Business Review*, April 2002, https://hbr.org/2002/04/wealth-happens.

2. Andrea Stephenson, Justin W. Adams, and Mauro Vaccarezza, "The Vertebrate Heart: An Evolutionary Perspective," *Journal of Anatomy* 231, no. 6 (2017): 787–97, https://onlinelibrary.wiley.com/doi/10.1111/joa.12687.

3. Michael Rothschild, *Bionomics: The Inevitability of Capitalism* (New York: Henry Holt, 1990), 117–26.

4. Rothschild, *Bionomics*, 127–40.

5. Jack Henningfield and David T. Sweanor, "A Social and Cultural History of Smoking," Britannica, accessed December 30, 2023, https://www.britannica.com/topic/smoking-tobacco/A-social-and-cultural-history-of-smoking.

6. "A Look at How Big Tobacco Infiltrated Baseball," *Truth Initiative*, June 9, 2023, https://truthinitiative.org/research-resources/tobacco-industry-marketing/look-how-big-tobacco-infiltrated-baseball.

7. Phil Edwards, "What Everyone Gets Wrong about the History of Cigarettes," *Vox*, April 6, 2015, https://www.vox.com/2015/3/18/8243707/cigarette-rolling-machines.

8. Casey Ashlock, "A Brief History of Cigarette Cards," *GoCollect*, April 12, 2021, https://blog.gocollect.com/a-brief-history-of-cigarette-cards/.

9. "Clearing the Smoke: Assessing the Science Base for Tobacco Harm Reduction," *National Library of Medicine*, accessed August 17, 2024, https://www.ncbi.nlm.nih.gov/books/NBK222369/

10. "Cultivation of a Tobacco Empire," *North Carolina Historic Sites,* accessed October 19, 2022, https://historicsites.nc.gov/all-sites/duke-homestead/history/cultivation-tobacco-empire.

11. Buckner F. Melton Jr, "Tobacco Litigation Trials: 1954-Present," Encyclopedia, October 19, 2022, https://www.encyclopedia.com/law/law-magazines/tobacco-litigation-trials-1954-present.

12. Amy Tikkamen, "American Tobacco Company," Britannica, accessed October 19, 2022, https://www.britannica.com/topic/American-Tobacco-Company.

13. "Primary Source: Working in a Tobacco Factory," *NCpedia*, accessed October 19, 2022, reprinted from "Long Record for Steady Work Held by Woman Who Began Her Duties in Duke's First Factory," *Durham Morning Herald,* January 17, 1926, https://www.ncpedia.org/anchor/working-tobacco-factory.

14. "A New Product," *Duke Homestead Education and History Corporation*, accessed October 19, 2022, https://dukehomestead.org/duke-family-history/.

15. Kayleen Devlin, "Meet The Fakers Of Nature," *BBC Earth*, accessed August 14, 2024, https://www.bbcearth.com/news/meet-the-fakers-of-nature

16. M. T. Wroblewski, "What Is Puffery in Advertising?" *Chron*, September 17, 2020, https://smallbusiness.chron.com/puffery-advertising-24357.html.

17. Tejvan Pettinger, "Profit Maximisation," *Economics Help*, July 16, 2019, https://www.economicshelp.org/blog/3201/economics/profit-maximisation/.

18. Chad Stone, Danilo Trisi, Arloc Sherman, and Jennifer Beltrán, "A Guide to Statistics on Historical Trends in Income Inequality," *Center on Budget and Policy Priorities*, updated January 13, 2020, https://www.cbpp.org/research/poverty-and-inequality/a-guide-to-statistics-on-historical-trends-in-income-inequality.

19. Peter J. Boettke, Peter T. Leeson, and Daniel J. Smith, "The Evolution of Economics: Where We Are and How We Got Here," Peterlesson, accessed June 28, 2024, https://www.peterleeson.com/The_Evolution_of_Economics.pdf.

20. Aaron O'Neill, "Estimated Global Population from 10,000 BCE to 2100," *Statista*, updated July 4, 2024, https://www.statista.com/statistics/1006502/global-population-ten-thousand-bc-to-2050/.

21. Robert B. Reich, "How Capitalism Is Killing Democracy," *Foreign Policy*, October 12, 2009, https://foreignpolicy.com/2009/10/12/how-capitalism-is-killing-democracy/.

Chapter 16

1. Bernd Heinrich, *Bumblebee Economics* (Cambridge, MA: Harvard University Press, 1979, 2004), 142.

2. Michael Rothschild, *Bionomics: The Inevitability of Capitalism (New York: Henry Holt, 1990)*, 155–64.

3. "Smoking and Agriculture: The Toll of Tobacco on Farmers and the Planet," *Tobacco Free Life*, accessed June 28, 2024, https://tobaccofreelife.org/resources/smoking-agriculture/.

4. "Smoking and Cancer," *CDC*, October 13, 2023, https://www.cdc.gov/tobacco/campaign/tips/diseases/cancer.html.

5. "Health Effects of Secondhand Smoke," *American Lung Association*, June 25, 2024, https://www.lung.org/quit-smoking/smoking-facts/health-effects/secondhand-smoke.

6. J. Robert Branston, "Industry Profits Continue to Drive the Tobacco Epidemic: A New Endgame for Tobacco Control?" *Tobacco Prevention & Cessation* 7, no. 6 (2021): 45, https://www.tobaccopreventioncessation.com/Industry-profits-continue-to-drive-the-tobacco-epidemic-A-new-endgame-

for-tobacco,138232,0,2.html.

7. Ron Elving, "The NRA Wasn't Always Against Gun Restrictions," *NPR*, October 10, 2017, https://www.npr.org/2017/10/10/556578593/the-nra-wasnt-always-against-gun-restrictions.

8. "What Is a PAC?" *Open Secrets*, accessed October 20, 2022, https://www.opensecrets.org/political-action-committees-pacs/what-is-a-pac.

9. Adam Smith, *The Wealth of Nations, Books I–III* (London: Penguin Books, 1776, 1999), 167–90.

10. Elias Beck, "Working Conditions in the Industrial Revolution," *History Crunch*, updated March 25, 2022, https://www.historycrunch.com/working-conditions-in-the-industrial-revolution.html#/.

11. Mark Meredith, "Marble House," House HisTree, updated September 19, 2022, https://househistree.com/houses/marble-house.

12. US Department of Labor, "5. Progressive Era Investigations," *US Department of Labor*, accessed October 20, 2022, https://www.dol.gov/general/aboutdol/history/mono-regsafepart05.

Chapter 17

1. Miguel Douglas, "Native Americans Are Not All the Same: An Exploration of Indigenous Diversity," *American Indian Republic*, October 22, 2021, https://americanindianrepublic.com/native-americans-are-not-all-the-same-an-exploration-of-indigenous-diversity/.

2. Jacques Barzun, *From Dawn to Decadence: 1500 to the Present* (New York: Harper Collins, 2000), 3–20.

3. Editors of Encyclopedia Britannica, "Kurd," Britannica, last updated July 15, 2024, https://www.britannica.com/topic/Kurd.

4. E. A. Thompson, "Attila King of the Huns," Britannica, accessed May 7, 2024, https://www.britannica.com/biography/Attila-king-of-the-Huns.

Chapter 18

1. Susan Brink, "What Happens to the Body and Mind When Starvation Sets In?" *NPR,* January 20, 2016, https://www.npr.org/sections/what-happens-to-the-body-and-mind-when-starvation-sets-in.

2. Chad Stone, Danilo Trisi, Arloc Sherman, and Jennifer Beltrán, "A Guide to Statistics on Historical Trends in Income

Inequality," *Center on Budget and Policy Priorities*, updated January 13, 2020, https://www.cbpp.org/research/poverty-and-inequality/a-guide-to-statistics-on-historical-trends-in-income-inequality.

3. Gregory Alexander and Charles Donahue, "Property Law and the Western Concept of Private Property," Britannica, October 20, 2022, https://www.britannica.com/topic/property-law/Property-law-and-the-Western-concept-of-private-property.

4. Maria S. Cox, Fritz Neumark, and Charles E. McLure, "Taxation," Britannica, updated June 28, 2024, https://www.britannica.com/topic/taxation.

5. "The Constitution of the United States: A Transcription," *National Archives*, accessed October 20, 2022, https://www.archives.gov/founding-docs/constitution-transcript.

Chapter 20

1. eLaw Talk, "9 of the Most Common Types of Government Systems Explained," *elawtalk*, January 10, 2022, https://elawtalk.com/types-of-government-systems/.

2. Bill Keller, "Major Soviet Paper Says 20 Million Died As Victims of Stalin," *The New York Times*, February 4, 1989, https://www.nytimes.com/1989/02/04/world/major-soviet-paper-says-20-million-died-as-victims-of-stalin.html.

3. Scott Kennedy and Jude Blanchette, "Chinese State Capitalism," *Center for Strategic & International Studies*, October 7, 2021, https://www.csis.org/analysis/chinese-state-capitalism.

4. "The Constitution of the United States: A Transcription," *National Archives*, accessed October 20, 2022, https://www.archives.gov/founding-docs/constitution-transcript.

5. "Lobbying Data Summary," *Open Secrets*, accessed July 5, 2024, https://www.opensecrets.org/federal-lobbying.

6. Karl Evers-Hillstrom, "Most Expensive Ever: 2020 Election Cost $14.4 Billion," *Open Secrets*, February 11, 2021, https://www.opensecrets.org/news/2021/02/2020-cycle-cost-14-billion/.

7. Michael Rothschild, *Bionomics: The Inevitability of Capitalism (New York: Henry Holt, 1990)*, 91–98.

8. Wendy Sawyer and Peter Wagner, "Mass Incarceration: The Whole Pie 2023," *Prison Policy Initiative*, March 14, 2023, https://www.prisonpolicy.org/reports/pie2023.html.

9. Fausto Petrelli et al., "Association of Obesity with Survival Outcomes in Patients with Cancer: A Systematic Review and Meta-Analysis," *JAMA Network Open 4, no. 3* (2021): e13520, https://jamanetwork.com/journals/jamanetworkopen/fullarticle/2777839.

10. Rothschild, *Bionomics*, 141–52.

11. "Amazon.com, Inc. (AMZN)," *Stock Analysis*, accessed July 5, 2024, https://stockanalysis.com/stocks/amzn/.

12. Robin Hartill, CFP, "The Definitive Guide: How to Value a Stock," *The Motley Fool*, updated November 13, 2023, https://www.fool.com/investing/how-to-invest/stocks/how-to-value-stock/.

13. Oren M. Levin-Waldman, "How Inequality Undermines Democracy," *E-International Relations*, December 10, 2016, https://www.e-ir.info/2016/12/10/how-inequality-undermines-democracy/.

14. Rothschild, *Bionomics*, 54–71.

15. "United Nations Charter," *United Nations*, accessed July 5, 2024, https://www.un.org/en/about-us/un-charter.

16. "The Effects of Climate Change," *NASA*, accessed October 22, 2022, https://climate.nasa.gov/effects/.

Appendix 1

1. Ana Gutiérrez-Preciado, Hector Romero, and Mariana Peimbert, "An Evolutionary Perspective on Amino Acids," *Nature Education* 3, no. 9 (2010): 29, https://www.nature.com/scitable/topicpage/an-evolutionary-perspective-on-amino-acids-14568445/.

2. Uma Shanker, Brij Bhushan, G. Bhattacharjee, and Kamaluddin, "Formation of Nucleobases from Formamide in the Presence of Iron Oxides: Implication in Chemical Evolution and Origin of Life," *Astrobiology* 11, no. 3 (2011): 225–33, https://www.liebertpub.com/doi/abs/10.1089/ast.2010.0530.

3. Irene A. Chen and Peter Walde, "From Self-Assembled Vesicles to Protocells," *Cold Spring Harbor Perspectives in Biology* 2, no. 7 (2010): a002170, doi:10.1101/cshperspect.a002170, https://www.ncbi.nlm.nih.gov/pmc/articles/PMC2890201/.

4. Annabelle Biscans, "Exploring the Emergence of RNA Nucleosides and Nucleotides on the Early Earth," *Life (Basel)* 8, no. 4 (2018): 57, doi:10.3390/life8040057, https://www.ncbi.nlm.nih.gov/pmc/articles/PMC6316623/.

5. James Trefil, *1001 Things Everyone Should Know About Science* (New York: Doubleday, 1992), 80.

6. Ying-Wei Yang, Su Zhang, Elizabeth O. McCullum, and John C. Chaput, "Experimental Evidence That GNA and TNA Were Not Sequential Polymers in the Prebiotic Evolution of RNA," *Journal of Molecular Evolution* 65, no. 3 (2007): 289–95, https://pubmed.ncbi.nlm.nih.gov/17828568/.

7. David Wang and Aisha Farhana, "Biochemistry, RNA Structure," in *StatPearls* (Treasure Island, FL: StatPearls Publishing; 2022), https://www.ncbi.nlm.nih.gov/books/NBK558999/.

8. Ruairi J. Mackenzie, "DNA vs. RNA—5 Key Differences and Comparison," *Technology Networks—Genomic Research*, updated January 22, 2024, https://www.technologynetworks.com/genomics/lists/what-are-the-key-differences-between-dna-and-rna-296719.

9. Bruce Alberts et al., "The RNA World and the Origins of Life," in *Molecular Biology of the Cell, 4th ed.* (New York: Garland Science, 2002), https://www.ncbi.nlm.nih.gov/books/NBK26876/.

10. Bruce Alberts et al., "From DNA to RNA," in *Molecular Biology of the Cell, 4th ed.* (New York: Garland Science, 2002), https://www.ncbi.nlm.nih.gov/books/NBK26887/

11. Reginald Davey, "What Is a Protocell?" *AZO Life Sciences*, accessed September 23, 2022, https://www.azolifesciences.com/article/What-is-a-Protocell.aspx.

12. Norio Kitadai and Shigenori Maruyama, "Origins of Building Blocks of Life: A Review," *Geoscience Frontiers* 9, no. 4 (2018): 1117–53, https://www.sciencedirect.com/science/article/pii/S1674987117301305

13. Alberts et al., "From DNA to RNA."

14. Leslie A. Pray, "DNA Replication and Causes of Mutation," *Nature Education* 1, no. 1 (2008): 214, https://www.nature.com/scitable/topicpage/dna-replication-and-causes-of-mutation.

Appendix 2

1. Wex Definitions Team, "Freedom of Speech," *Cornell Law School*, June 2021, https://www.law.cornell.edu/wex/freedom_of_speech.

2. Purdue Online Writing Lab, "Journalism and Journalistic Writing: Introduction," *Purdue University*, accessed July 5, 2024, https://owl.purdue.edu/owl/subject_specific_writing/journalism_and_journalistic_writing/index.html.

3. "SPJ Code of Ethics," *Society of Professional Journalists*, September 6, 2014, https://www.spj.org/ethicscode.asp.

4. "A Brief History of Fake News," *Center for Information Technology & Society, UC Santa Barbara*, accessed July 5, 2024, https://cits.ucsb.edu/fake-news/brief-history.

5. Office of the Historian, "US Diplomacy and Yellow Journalism, 1895–1898," *US Department of State*, accessed July 5, 2024, https://history.state.gov/milestones/1866-1898/yellow-journalism#.

6. Matt Stefon, "Fairness Doctrine," Britannica, May 21, 2024, https://www.britannica.com/topic/Fairness-Doctrine.

7. Jonathan Edwards, "Bus-Riding Dog Who Took Herself to Park Remembered as 'Seattle Icon,'" *The Washington Post*, October 18, 2022, https://www.washingtonpost.com/nation/2022/10/18/eclipse-bus-riding-dog-dies/.

Afterword

This was not an easy book to read for any number of reasons. This book is designed for non-scientists, and though I have gone to great lengths to simplify the scientific ideas included in this book, they are still scientific ideas that can be hard to wrap your head around when you're not used to thinking of the world this way. Thank you for persevering.

In this book I have let the theory guide me to the answers to some of humanity's fundamental questions. To be honest, even I was surprised at where that led me, and I have found I have looked at some of my long-held beliefs in new ways.

I would be remiss if I did not mention the most influential thinkers that enabled me to develop the ideasphere theory.

First, Michael Rothschild who wrote *Bionomics - Economy as Ecosystem* in 1990. Rothschild thoughtfully detailed how economic systems mirror biological systems. It was a compelling, rich, and insightful book. I have been thinking about this book in one way or another since the year I first read it. Rothschild was brave. I think this was the first book to delve into the link between natural and human systems since the Social Darwinism fiasco of the late 1800's. Perhaps people have been afraid to link humanity to biology for fear of repeating the tendency to give people license to do horrible things and blame it on nature.

Rothschild showed that economic systems do indeed mirror natural behaviors. I am more than grateful for Rothschild's insights, but even reading *Bionomics* as a young adult, I couldn't help thinking that if economics mirrored biology, shouldn't all of humanity mirror biology? In fact, I was sure that within a year or two of the publication of *Bionomics*, someone would make this link. That book never came. Worse, the term bionomics was co-opted to measure the economic cost of climate change and other human activities. That is why I finally decided to write this book; the book I was waiting for.

Second, I am in awe of Charles Darwin. *The Origin of Species* is a tough read; Darwin wrote run on sentences on top of run on sentences. But what a thinker. I came away from each page astounded at his ability to reason through the ideas of evolution so clearly and compellingly using his experiments with beetles and bees and barnacles. And even as an introvert, he kept up with other scientists and their discoveries for years and years. Darwin's *The Voyage of the Beagle* is as compelling. Darwin wrote this book while he served as naturalist companion to the captain of the Beagle while it made a five-year voyage beginning in 1831. He was 22 years old. His observations and ability to work out how natural formations and living structures emerged are clearly evident in this book. It is apparent that this trip planted the idea of change in his mind early in his life and that evolution was the natural conclusion he drew from his observations.

Stephen Jay Gould's book, *Wonderful Life*, cemented the idea in my mind that change is the only constant in the universe, and that this Earth and the humans on it, are unlikely to even exist. That very improbability makes me, as it did Gould, more appreciative of our existence; and ever more incented to make sure humans stick around.

Last, the writers of the Constitution have my deep gratitude. They had the ability to put into practical form ideas about government they could not prove as right but which they intuitively understood to be true. They have come the closest to mirroring the lessons nature would teach us if it could. It is my fervent hope that 200 plus years after the founding of our nation, we will heed these lessons and will not let the brilliant ideas upon which our country is founded perish from this earth.

I give my thanks to the many professionals in the world today. Scientists and thinkers, economists and philosophers, sociologists and leaders and too many others to count. Though I am not of your ilk, and am far more a generalist than a specialist, it is in you that I put my hope for a better future. You study and learn the details of your respective professions and build the tools that allow us to live better lives. I hope that this book might provide you with a different context, with a new lens, so to speak, by which you can continue your work in a way that improves life on Earth.

Anne Riley
August 21, 2024

Acknowledgments

I am grateful for so many people who have helped me bring this book into reality, and to enable me to spread the word about the ideasphere. I am by nature an introvert, so spreading the word about a new idea is akin to torture, even when I think the idea is a good one. I am grateful to Jared Rosen from Dreamsculpt Books who planted the idea of re-writing my novel *DINA: Nature's Case For Democracy* into a serious non-fiction book. I put a few jokes in anyway; I couldn't help myself. Joyce Walker edited the manuscript and my numerous sources. As I'm not a scientist, I had to document even basic information, so that was a big job. Thank you. Juliet Clark is my go-to marketing specialist and publisher. She makes me do non-introvert stuff I don't want to do and is even nice about it.

I want to thank my son-in-law Greg Brennecka, a bona fide scientist, who reviewed an early version of the book and gave me really great pointers in how to make the book more approachable. My sister, Mary Voiland, has been a champion of the ideasphere concept. She is the one who holds my hand when I despair that I am just spitting into the wind as I try to encourage people to think an entirely new way. After reading *DINA*, she said to me, "I want to help change the world. What can I do?" She is the kindest person I